PLAB

PART 1 EMQ

POCKET BOOK 4

PASTEST
Dedicated to your success

PLAB
PART 1 EMQ
POCKET BOOK 4

Julia Harris MB ChB(Hons) FRCS FFAEM

Consultant in Emergency Medicine
Southampton General Hospital
Southampton

Patrick Roberts FRCS Ed

Specialist Registrar, Emergency Department
Chelsea and Westminster Hospital
London

Andrew Saich BSc(Hons) MRCP

Honorary Registrar in Emergency Medicine
Chelsea and Westminster Hospital
London

PASTEST
Dedicated to your success

Egerton Court, Parkgate Estate,
Knutsford, Cheshire, WA16 8DX
Telephone: 01565 752000

First edition 2004

A catalogue record for this book is available from the British Library.

ISBN: 1 904627 06 4

Typeset by Breeze Limited, Manchester
Printed and bound in Great Britain by MPG Books Ltd, Bodmin, Cornwall

CONTENTS

INTRODUCTION

Welcome to another PLAB EMQ preparation book.

The format of the book is as would be found in a single PLAB Part 1 examination. There are 200 extended match questions for you to work through with answers and explanations at the back of the book.

Preferences for exam preparation vary – some candidates like to work through as many questions as possible and use that as a focus for subsequent revision, others pre-read subject areas and dip into EMQ books or you may wish to use this book to work through 'under exam conditions' in three hours to assess your performance and progress. The timing in the examination is tight with less that one minute per question. It is useful to practice this timing. The examination is not negatively marked and failure to answer all questions is a missed opportunity.

The standard of the examination is that required to ensure successful candidates are able to perform at Senior House Officer level in the NHS. The skills tested are those achieved through study and clinical experience.

The pass mark will vary with each sitting. The minimum score for success is likely to be in the region of 50–60%.

We wish you success in your examination. Good luck.

NORMAL VALUES

SERUM	NORMAL RANGE
Albumin	36–52 g/l
Amylase	70–300 U/l
Bicarbonate	22–28 mmol/l
Bilirubin	5–20 µmol/l
Calcium	2.20–2.60 mmol/l
Chloride	95–105 mmol/l
Creatinine kinase	23–175 U/l
Creatinine	60–120 µmol/l
D-Dimer	< 0.3 mg/l
Gamma-glutamyltransferase (GGT)	< 40 U/l
Globulins	24–37 g/l
Immunoglobulins	
IgG	5.3–16.5 g/l
IgA	0.8–4.0 g/l
IgM	0.5–2.0 g/l
Iron	14–29 µmol/l
Iron binding capacity (TIBC)	45–75 µmol/l
Lactate dehydrogenase (LDH)	100–300 U/l
Magnesium	0.70–1.00 mmol/l
Osmolality	270–295 mmol/l
Phosphatase (acid)	0–4 U/l
Phosphatase (alkaline)	40–115 U/l
Phosphate	0.8–1.4 mmol/l
Potassium	3.5–5.0 mmol/l
Protein	62–82 g/l
Sodium	135–145 mmol/l
Thyroid function tests	
T_4	54–144 nmol/l
TSH	0.10–5.0 mU/l
T_3	0.8–2.7 nmol/l
FT_4	9–25 pmol/l
TBG	10–30 mg/l
Transaminase ALT	11–55 U/l
Transaminase AST	13–42 U/l
Transferrin	2–4 g/l
Urate	0.24–0.45 mmol/l
Urea	2.5–6.6 mmol/l

PLASMA

Glucose	3.0–5.9 mmol/l
Arterial blood gases	
[H^+]	36–43 nmol/l
P_{CO_2}	4.6–6.0 kPa
Bicarbonate	20–28 mmol/l
P_{O_2}	10.5–13.5 kPa
Lactate	0.63–2.44 mmol/l
Pyruvate	34–80 μmol/l

CEREBROSPINAL FLUID (CSF)

Glucose	2.5–3.9 mmol/l
Protein	< 0.45 g/l

URINE

Catecholamines	< 1.3 mmol/24 h
VMA (HMMA)	9–36 μmol/24 h
5HIAA	10–50 μmol/24 h
Creatinine clearance	60–110 ml/min

MISCELLANEOUS

Faecal fat	< 10 mmol/24 h
Xylose excretion test	
Urine excretion (25 g dose)	> 33 mmol/5 h
Urine excretion (5 g dose)	> 8 mmol/5 h
Blood xylose at 1 h (25 g dose)	2.0–4.8 mmol/l
Blood xylose at 2 h (25 g dose)	1.0–5.0 mmol/l

ABBREVIATIONS

ACE	angiotensin-converting enzyme
ACTH	adrenocorticotrophic hormone
AST	aspartate transaminase
AV	atriovenous
AV	atrioventricular
BP	blood pressure
Bpm	beats per minute
BTS	British Thoracic Society
CK	creatinine kinase
CPR	cardiopulmonary resuscitation
CRP	C-reactive protein
CSF	cerebrospinal fluid
CT	computed tomography
CVP	central venous pressure
EBV	Epstein-Barr virus
ECG	electrocardiogram
ENT	ear, nose, throat
ESR	erythrocyte sedimentation rate
GCS	Glasgow Coma Scale
GI	gastrointestinal
GP	General Practitioner
HONK	hyperosmolar non-ketotic coma
INR	international normalised ratio
IUCD	intrauterine contraceptive device
JVP	jugular venous pressure
MCV	mean corpuscular volume
MRI	magnetic resonance imaging
NIDDM	non-insulin-dependent diabetes mellitus
NSAID	non-steriodal anti-inflammatory drugs
PE	pulmonary embolism
PEA	pulseless electrical activity
PEFR	peak expiratory flow rate
SAH	subarachnoid haemorrhage
SHO	senior house officer
SLE	systemic lupus erythematosus
SVT	supraventricular tachycardia
VF	ventricular failure
VT	ventricular tachycardia
WCC	white blood cell count

EMQ EXAMINATION TECHNIQUE FOR THE PLAB TEST

The Extended Matching Question Paper in the PLAB exam consists of 200 'Items' (questions) to be answered in three hours, in other words you have 54 seconds in which to answer each question.

Each EMQ consists of the following:

- A Theme: This tells you what the question is about, in terms of both the clinical problem area e.g. 'Causes of swollen leg (s)' and the skill required e.g. 'investigation'. (see example below).
- A list of Options: The options or answers are listed in alphabetical order (see example below).
- An Instruction: This precedes the numbered items and explains what you should do to answer the question. The 'instruction' is very similar throughout the exam paper and typically reads: 'For each scenario below, choose the SINGLE most discriminating investigation from the list of options'.
- A set of Items: Within each theme there are several numbered items, usually between four and six. These are the questions/problems that you have to solve (see the example below).

The example opposite illustrates the structure of a typical EMQ:

1. Theme: Causes of swollen leg(s)

Options:

A	Cellulitis	F	Lymphoedema
B	Deep vein thrombosis	G	Venous incompetence
C	Congestive cardiac failure	H	Torn gastrocnemius muscle
D	Hypoalbuminaemia	I	Elephantiasis
E	Ruptured Baker's cyst	J	Milroy's syndrome

Instruction:
For each patient below, choose the SINGLE most likely diagnosis from the above list of options. Each option may be used once, more than once, or not at all.

Items:

1. A 50-year-old woman has bilateral swollen red legs. She has had previous surgery to both legs for varicose veins. On examination she has pitting oedema and varicose eczema. The legs are not tender.

2. A 60-year-old man has swollen legs and distended abdomen. He has a history of excess alcohol intake. He is mildly jaundiced with spider naevi on his face. His abdomen is dull to percussion in the flanks.

3. A 35-year-old pregnant woman has developed a swollen left leg over the last 36 hours. It is painful, red and hot. Temperature is 37.8°C.

4. A 42-year-old woman has gross swelling of the whole of both legs. Her skin is dry and appears crusty. She has previously had radiotherapy for cervical cancer.

5. A 52-year-old man with diabetes has a two-day history of increasing pain and swelling in his left leg and sweats. On examination is pyrexial 38.5°C and his lower leg is tense, tender, hot and erythematous.

6. A 38-year-old woman with rheumatoid arthritis suddenly developed pain behind her right knee followed by pain and swelling of her right calf. On examination, she is apyrexial and has a tender swelling of her upper calf.

How to attempt the EMQs

- It is important that you begin by carefully reading the instruction which precedes the numbered items.

- Then consider each of the numbered items and decide what you think the answer is for each item. You should then look for the answer in the list of options. If you cannot find the answer you have thought of, you should look for the option, which in your opinion, is the best answer to the problem.

- For each numbered item, you must choose ONE and only one of the options. You may feel that there are several possible answers to an item, but you must choose the one most likely from the option list. If you enter more than one answer on the answer sheet you will gain no mark for the question even though you may have given the right answer along with one or more wrong ones.

- In each theme there are more options than items, so not all the options will be used as answers. This is why the instruction says that some options may not be used at all.

- A given option may provide the answer to more than one item. For example, there might be two items which contain descriptions of patients, and the most likely diagnosis could be the same in both instances. In this case the option can be used more than once.

- You will be awarded one mark for each item answered correctly. Marks are not deducted for incorrect answers nor for failure to answer. The total score on the paper is the number of correct answers given. You should, therefore, attempt all items.

Marking your answer sheet

The answer sheet will be read by an automatic document reader which transfers the information it reads to a computer. It must therefore be filled out in accordance with the instructions. Record your answers by making a heavy black line in the appropriate block on the answer sheet by using the pencil provided in the examination hall. Each block correctly filled in scores +1.

With 200 questions to answer in three hours this means 54 seconds per question for thinking time *and* marking the computer answer sheet. Do not waste precious time at the official exam in familiarising yourself with the computer boxes and how to mark them, you must practice this beforehand on the sheet provided.

Read all the official information from the General Medical Council with great care and make sure that you understand the instructions. Some candidates like to mark their answer sheet as they go through the test and others like to mark their question papers and leave time at the end to transfer marks to the answer sheet. If you decide to mark your answers first of all on the question paper then it is vital that you leave enough time to transfer your answers onto the computer sheet before the end of the allowed time of three hours. You will not be given extra time at the exam in which to transfer your marks onto the computer sheet.

If you are not sure about a particular answer (for example question 14) and wish to return to it at the end, be sure that you do not mark the answer to 15 in the empty boxes relating the question 14. You can put a tiny mark against the number on your answer sheet indicating that you wish to return and this will remind you to leave it blank so you can return to it at the end.

Careless marking of the printed answer sheet is probably one of the commonest causes of rejection by the document reader. You must fill in the blocks on the official answer sheet as strongly and neatly as you can.

To guess or not to guess

If you cannot find the answer you have thought of in the list of options, you should look for the option which, in your opinion, is the best answer to the problem. Candidates are frequently uncertain whether or not to guess the answer. However, it is in your best interest to answer every question on this paper as the exam is not negatively marked, therefore, even if you are unsure it is worth your best guess. To repeat the most important points of technique:

1. Read the instruction very carefully and be sure you understand it.
2. Use reasoning to work out your answers.
3. If you are unsure of an answer make an educated guess.

4. BUT remember for EACH numbered item you must choose ONE, and only one, of the options.

5. Don't forget that it is possible for each option to be used once, more than once, or not at all.

6. Do not spend too long on problem questions, move on and come back to them when you have completed the rest if the paper.

7. Mark your responses clearly, correctly and accurately.

8. Keep an eye on your clock and be sure to complete the paper before the end of three hours.

EMQ PRACTICE EXAMINATION

200 questions: time allowed 3 hours

Theme: Upper abdominal pain

Options

A Bleeding peptic ulcer
B Biliary colic
C Cholecystitis
D Gastric outlet syndrome
E Lower lobe pneumonia
F Myocardial infarction
G Pancreatitis
H Perforated peptic ulcer
I Ulcerative colitis

For each of the scenarios below select the SINGLE most likely diagnosis from the above list of options. Each option may be used once, more than once, or not at all.

1. A 33-year-old woman presents with severe abdominal pain radiating to the back. She is shocked and hyperventilating. There is no free gas on her erect chest X-ray. An opacity is noted at the level of the L1 vertebra.

2. A 57-year-old smoker presents with epigastric pain, sweating and is vomiting clear fluid. He has a pulse of 58 bpm and a high JVP.

3. A 43-year-old man with multiple sclerosis presents with pulse of 120 and a rigid abdomen. He is apyrexial. There are no bowel sounds. He has recently completed a course of methylprednisolone.

4. A 47-year-old woman presents with intermittent epigastric pain and vomiting. When present, the pain may last for hours. She has mild epigastric and right upper quadrant tenderness. Bowel sounds are present.

5. An 83-year-old man presents following a collapse. He is not tachycardic but has a postural drop in blood pressure. He has mild epigastric discomfort. You note he has a history of arthritis and hypertension.

Theme: Painful upper limb

Options

A Anterior dislocaton of the shoulder
B de Quervain's tenosynovitis
C Colles' fracture
D Fractured surgical neck of humerus
E Gamekeeper's thumb
F Posterior dislocaton of the shoulder
G Scaphoid fracture
H Supracondylar fracture of the humerus
I Smith's fracture

For each of the scenarios below select the SINGLE most likely diagnosis from the above list of options. Each option may be used once, more than once, or not at all.

6. A 23-year-old man complains of a painful wrist after falling over whilst drunk. There is tenderness in the thenar eminence and pain abducting his thumb.

7. A 4-year-old girl presents with a painful swollen arm after falling off a pony. The nurse experiences difficulty taking the radial pulse.

8. A 35-year-old electrician is brought in with a painful upper limb and chest pain following an accident at work in which he received an electric shock.

9. A 67-year-old woman fell while out shopping. She is clutching her arm to her side and complaining of pain.

10. A 31-year-old factory worker complains of a painful arm. She attends late at night because of difficulty sleeping. There is swelling on the radial side of her forearm above the wrist, with crepitus felt on movement at this site.

Theme: Carcinogenesis

Options

A	Aflatoxins	E	Cadmium
B	Aniline dyes	F	Epstein–Barr virus (EBV)
C	Asbestos	G	Oestrogens
D	Azo dyes	H	Vinyl chloride

For each of the diseases below indicate the associated carcinogenic agent from the above list of options. Each option may be used once, more than once, or not at all.

11. Bladder cancer.

12. Angiosarcoma of the liver.

13. Mesothelioma.

14. Carcinoma of the prostate.

15. Endometrial carcinoma.

Theme: Causes of collapse in a woman who is 35 weeks' pregnant

Options

A	Amniotic fluid embolism	E	Placental abruption
B	Anaphylactic shock	F	Pulmonary embolism
C	Aortocaval compression	G	Septicaemia
D	Pre-eclampsia	H	Vasovagal syncope

For each of the scenarios below give the SINGLE most likely diagnosis from the above list of options. Each option may be used once, more than once, or not at all.

16. A gravida-6 para-5 woman with episodes of nocturnal dizziness which have begun to occur during the day.

17. A 23-year-old primagravida found collapsed at home by her husband. She has refused all antenatal care. She is drowsy and complaining of headache.

18. A 35-year-old woman with a recent history of watery vaginal discharge. She is tachycardic and flushed, with a wide pulse pressure.

19. A gravida-2 para-1 woman presents with collapse and severe abdominal pain. Examination reveals a hard uterus with no signs of labour.

20. A 43-year-old woman presents following collapse at home. She is cyanosed and is noted to be in active labour.

Theme: Biochemistry of jaundice

Options

A	Dubin–Johnson syndrome	E	Intrahepatic cholestasis
B	Extrahepatic cholestasis	F	Long-term tricyclic antidepressant use
C	Gilbert's syndrome		
D	Haemolytic jaundice		

For each of the following choose the SINGLE most likely diagnosis from the above list of options. Each option may be used once, more than once, or not at all.

21. Mildly elevated serum bilirubin, normal haemoglobin, normal alkaline phosphatase, normal serum aspartate transaminase (AST). No urinary bilirubin.

22. Elevated serum bilirubin with a very elevated alkaline phosphatase. Minimally elevated AST. Bilirubin in the urine. Normal haemoglobin.

23. Elevated serum bilirubin with a mildly elevated alkaline phosphatase and a very elevated AST. Bilirubin in the urine. Normal haemoglobin.

24. Mildly elevated serum bilirubin, anaemia, normal alkaline phosphatase and AST. No urinary bilirubin.

Theme: Death in hospital

Options

A	Appropriately trained senior nurse to certify death	F	Final-year medical student locum to certify death
B	Appropriately trained senior nurse to verify death	G	General Practitioner (GP) to issue death certificate
C	Certification of death in notes	H	Issue death certificate
D	Complete Part 1 of cremation form	I	Paramedic to certify death
E	Coroner to issue death certificate	J	Verification of death in notes

For each of the following cases indicate the SINGLE most appropriate course of action from the above list of options. You are a Senior House Officer (SHO). Each option may be used once, more than once, or not at all.

25. On your first day back from annual leave you are called to the ward to see a patient who has died. She was admitted the previous evening for terminal care.

26. An elderly man dies on the ward following a long illness. You are assisting in the operating theatre and cannot go to the ward. The nursing staff indicate that the patient in the adjacent bed is distressed about the death and the patient cannot be moved to the mortuary until death has been confirmed. You have a final-year medical student covering the wards.

27. A 27-year-old man dies two days after routine surgery. You have been involved with his peri-operative care. He has been certified as dead in the notes by your House Officer.

28. A 67-year-old man is referred for admission by his GP for a presumed myocardial infarction. He has a history of hypertension and angina. He is a smoker. On arrival he is in cardiac arrest. Resuscitation is unsuccessful. You arrive after the Emergency Department doctor has certified death.

29. An elderly woman is admitted following a road traffic accident. She sustained a fractured left (dominant) wrist and soft tissue injuries. She dies five days later of a cardiac dysrhythmia.

Theme: Vaginal bleeding

Options

- A Carcinoma of the cervix
- B Ectopic pregnancy
- C Endometrial carcinoma
- D Inevitable abortion
- E Mirena intrauterine contraceptive device (IUCD)
- F Missed abortion
- G Normal menstruation
- H Threatened abortion
- I Uterine fibroids

For each of the cases below indicate the SINGLE most likely diagnosis from the above list of options. Each option may be used once, more than once, or not at all.

30. A 27-year-old woman presents with ten weeks' amenorrhoea, breast tenderness and a recent onset of low abdominal pain. She has a heavy vaginal bleed. On examination there are blood clots in the vagina and the cervical os is open.

31. A 38-year-old woman presents with painless post-coital bleeding. She had a cone biopsy for carcinoma in situ five years ago. Her last smear was three months ago, following this. Her last period was six weeks ago.

32. A 49-year-old woman presents with vaginal bleeding. Her last period was 18 months ago and her last smear was five months ago. Uterine curettage and ultrasound tests are normal.

33. A 40-year-old woman presents with menorrhagia. Bimanual examination reveals a bulky uterus.

34. A 22-year-old woman presents with a ten-week history of amenorrhoea and a painless, light, brown vaginal loss. Vaginal examination reveals an orange-sized uterus and no adnexal tenderness. The cervical os is closed.

Theme: Sexually transmitted diseases

Options

A	Candidiasis	F	Lymphogranuloma venereum
B	*Chlamydia trachomatis*	G	Primary syphilis
C	Gonorrhoea	H	Secondary syphilis
D	Herpes simplex virus	I	Trichomonal vaginosis
E	Human papilloma virus		

For each scenario below chose the SINGLE most likely diagnosis from the above list of options. Each option may be used once, more than once, or not at all.

35. Offensive, profuse, green-grey vaginal discharge in a 28-year-old woman. No visible lesions on speculum examination.

36. Painless indurated ulcer on the penis of a 35-year-old man. Smear from the ulcer base is positive to dark-field examination.

37. Small painless vulval ulcer in a 29-year-old woman who presents with enlarged lymph nodes in the groin. There are sinuses from the matted nodes.

38. A 24-year-old woman presents with painful urinary retention. She has clusters of small ulcers on the vulva and around the urethra.

39. A 29-year-old man returns from holiday abroad complaining of a milky urethral discharge.

Theme: Discoloured urine

Options

A	Alkaptonuria	F	Porphyria
B	Ciprofloxacin	G	Quinine
C	Haemolysis	H	Rifampicin
D	Myoglobinuria	I	Subendocardial endocarditis
E	Pancreatic carcinoma	J	Urethral tumour

For each of the following scenarios resulting in the passage of discoloured urine select the SINGLE most likely diagnosis from the above list of options. Each option may be used once, more than once, or not at all.

40. A 22-year-old contact of meningococcal disease complains of red urine and pink contact lenses. She was given prophylactic medication by the Public Health Department physician following contact tracing.

41. A 68-year-old man presents complaining that his urine has recently become darker. He also comments that his stools are difficult to flush away.

42. A young man is brought to the Emergency Department in an agitated state, having collapsed at a rave. He is pyrexial and passes dark urine.

43. A 43-year-old man complains that he produces dark urine when he begins to pass urine, which then clears.

44. A 20-year-old woman is vomiting, with severe abdominal pain, following a routine general anaesthetic for correction of bat ears. A container of her urine has been sitting on the bedside cabinet for some time and is noted to be very dark.

Theme: Urgent investigations of emergency presentations

Options

A	Biopsy	F	Serum analysis
B	Magnetic resonance imaging (MRI) scan	G	Spiral computed tomography (CT) scan
C	Percutaneous echocardiogram	H	Technetium-99m scan
D	Plain radiology	I	Ultrasound
E	Plain radiology with contrast		

For each of the following scenarios indicate the initial diagnostic investigation of choice from the above list of options. Each option may be used once, more than once, or not at all.

45. A 34-year-old man presents with the onset of testicular pain following a rugby match. On examination the testicle feels enlarged, with a small hydrocele. There is a history of orchidopexy in childhood.

46. A 5-year-old boy presents with a three-day history of ataxia and nystagmus. He is afebrile and has no other neurological signs. There is no history of toxin ingestion.

47. A 25-year-old woman presents with right-sided abdominal pain and rebound tenderness. Her last period was 26 days ago. She has white cells in her urine.

48. A 49-year-old man presents following a collapse on his way to work. Physical examination reveals a pulse of 120 bpm, temperature of 37.3 °C and a respiratory rate of 25/minute. ECG shows right axis deviation.

49. A 79-year-old woman presents with weak legs and urinary retention. She is taking tamoxifen and regular paracetamol for back pain.

Theme: Rheumatology

Options

A	Ankylosing spondylitis	F	Psoriatic arthropathy
B	Gouty arthritis	G	Reiter's disease
C	Osteoarthritis	H	Rheumatoid arthritis
D	Osteoporosis	I	Scleroderma
E	Polymyalgia rheumatica	J	Systemic lupus erthematosus

For each of the presentations described below, indicate the SINGLE most likely diagnosis from the above list of options. Each option may be used once, more than once, or not at all.

50. A 53-year-old woman has swan-neck deformities of her fingers and hip pain. X-ray examination reveals erosion of the ends of the phalanges.

51. A 23-year-old Afro-Caribbean woman presents with joint pains. She has a red facial rash. Examination of her hands appears normal.

52. A 56-year-old woman presents with knee and hip pain. X-rays of the hips show narrowing of the joint space and osteophyte formation. Examination of the knees demonstrates marked crepitus.

53. A 25-year-old man presents with a long history of low back pain. He is experiencing the acute onset of heel pain. Examination reveals tenderness beneath the calcaneum and a limited range of spinal movements.

54. An elderly woman complains of shoulder stiffness. She is unable to brush her hair or apply her make-up due to the stiffness. She denies true weakness. She attends with acute visual loss in the left eye.

Theme: Shock

Options

A	Anaphylactic shock	F	Septic shock
B	Cardiac tamponade	G	Shock lung
C	Cardiogenic shock	H	Tension pneumothorax
D	Haemorrhagic shock	I	Vasovagal shock
E	Neurogenic shock		

For each condition outlined below, indicate the SINGLE most likely shock syndrome from the above list of options. Each option may be used once, more than once, or not at all.

55. A 28-year-old man presents following a fall from a balcony. His pulse is 120 bpm, blood pressure 90/75 mmHg; he has cold peripheries, no fever, and oliguria. He groans on abdominal examination.

56. A 35-year-old woman presents following a motorcycle accident. Her pulse is 48 bpm, BP 95/40 mmHg; she has warm peripheries, is apyrexial and oliguric.

57. A 73-year-old woman is brought to the Emergency Department having been found at home by her home help. She has a pulse 110 bpm, BP 95/50 mmHg and warm peripheries. She is apyrexial. She has been incontinent of urine. Her home help hands you some antibiotics she has been taking.

58. A 29-year-old man with a history of drug abuse becomes unwell in the X-ray department 30 minutes after insertion of a CVP line for antibiotics. His pulse is 120 bpm, BP 90/68 mmHg; he has cold peripheries and distended neck veins.

59. A 56-year-old man presents with cyanosis, sweating, cold peripheries and severe chest pain. His ECG shows ST elevation in leads II, III and aVF. His pulse is 52/ bpm, BP 80/60 mmHg. He is apyrexial.

Theme: Facial pain

Options

A	Frontal sinusitis	F	Nasopharyngeal carcinoma
B	Herpes simplex	G	Parotid adenocarcinoma
C	Herpes zoster	H	Salivary duct stone
D	Ludwig's angina	I	Trigeminal neuralgia
E	Mumps	J	Vincent's angina

For each set of symptoms below give the SINGLE most likely diagnosis from the above list of options. Each option may be used once, more than once, or not at all.

60. Painful tender swelling of the floor of the mouth and upper neck.

61. Unilateral facial pain triggered by holding the telephone to the left ear in a patient with multiple sclerosis.

62. Painful swelling over the angle of the jaw and ipsilateral facial weakness.

63. Forehead pain and tenderness that becomes worse on leaning forwards.

64. Intermittent tender swelling beneath the jaw.

Theme: Acute red eye

Options

A	Acute glaucoma	F	Iritis
B	Central retinal vein occlusion	G	Keratitis
C	Viral conjunctivitis	H	Scleritis
D	Dacryadenitis	I	Trichiasis
E	Episcleritis		

For each clinical scenario below indicate the SINGLE most likely diagnosis from the above list of options. Each option may be used once, more than once, or not at all.

65. Bilateral itchy red eyes with profuse watery discharge. The tarsal conjunctiva reveals a follicular appearance. Normal visual acuity.

66. Painful red eye with a mucopurulent discharge. There is circum-corneal redness, with a hypopyon and a white opacity of the cornea.

67. Unilateral red eye with pain, photophobia and mild reduction in visual acuity, and a small pupil.

68. Severely painful red eye in an elderly man with reduced visual acuity, nausea and vomiting. The pupil is fixed and semi-dilated. There is intense engorgement of the corneal and episcleral vessels with corneal oedema.

69. Acute painful erythema limited to the inferolateral quadrant of the eye in a 35-year-old woman.

Theme: Post-traumatic pain relief

Options

A Fasciotomy
B Femoral nerve block
C Hanging cast
D Intramuscular NSAID
E Intramuscular opioids
F Intravenous diazepam
G Intravenous morphine
H Oral paracetamol
I Skin traction

For each of the following situations indicate the SINGLE most appropriate pain relief from the above list of options. Each option may be used once, more than once, or not at all.

70. A 27-year-old man has come off his motorbike. He has a Glasgow Coma Scale score of 13. He is otherwise stable but has a fractured shaft of femur.

71. A 25-year-old woman has sustained a recurrent dislocation of her left shoulder, falling off a horse. She has reduced this herself but complains of a painful left ankle, which is mildly swollen with no bony tenderness. She is four months pregnant.

72. A 93-year-old woman has a shortened, externally rotated left leg, having fallen out of bed in the ward. Her drug chart notes that she is allergic to pethidine.

73. A 43-year-old fireman has been brought in from a building where he jumped 15 feet from a window. He has bilateral severely painful heels and mid-back pain, but no other injuries.

74. A 58-year-old man is complaining of unrelieved pain in the left leg following application of a plaster cast for a fractured right tibia and fibula prior to surgery. The cast has been split and foot pulses are present. He last received an appropriate dose of morphine two hours ago.

Theme: Head injury

Options

A	Extradural haematoma	G	Subarachnoid haemorrhage
B	Acute subdural haematoma	H	Base of skull fracture
C	Depressed skull fracture	I	Contracoup injury
D	Hydrocephalus	J	Cerebral oedema
E	Sagittal sinus thrombosis	K	No intracerebral injury
F	Non-accidental injury		

For each scenario below indicate the SINGLE most likely diagnosis from the above list of options. Each option may be used once, more than once, or not at all.

75. A 22-year-old man presents with a decreased level of consciousness, having been found outside a nightclub. He has bruising of both eyes and a nosebleed. Skull X-ray reveals no fracture.

76. An 83-year-old woman has been hit by a car. She has been deeply unconscious since the accident. Skull X-rays are negative. CT scan shows an ellipse-shaped haematoma on the surface of the brain with midline shift to the opposite side.

77. A 3-month-old boy has been brought in fitting, with scalp swelling at the occiput. The history is that he rolled off the changing table whilst his nappy was being changed.

78. A 19-year-old rugby player hit his head on the post whist involved in a tackle. He was unconscious for five minutes but regained full consciousness and sat on the sideline until the end of the game. He was then noted to be drowsy and over the past 30 minutes has become confused and no longer obeys commands.

79. A 45-year-old salesman is brought in from a road traffic accident on the hard shoulder of the motorway. He was parked on the motorway when his vehicle was hit from behind by a van. He is deeply unconscious, with evidence of forehead and chest injuries. CT scan demonstrates frontal contusions and a large amount of blood in the basal cisterns.

Theme: Drug side-effects

Options

A Aciclovir
B Amoxicillin
C Bendroflumethiazide (bendrofluazide)
D Captopril
E Ciprofloxacin
F Erythromycin
G Furosemide (frusemide)
H Metformin
I Metoclopramide
J Oxytetracycline
K Rifampicin
L Ritonavir

From the list above select the drug MOST LIKELY to be involved in the cases described below. Each option may be used once, more than once, or not at all.

80. A 21-year-old girl seen recently by her GP presents to the Emergency Department with sore throat, lymphadenopathy, malaise and a new widespread erythematous rash.

81. A 68-year-old man, recently started on a new treatment by his GP, is brought into the Emergency Department having collapsed at home. He is found to have a blood pressure of 80/60 mmHg.

82. A 44-year-old HIV-positive man develops red urine on treatment for a chest condition.

83. An HIV-positive man with a low CD4 count develops severe upper abdominal pain while taking medication prescribed by the local hospital.

84. An 18-year-old girl complains of unsteadiness, headache and abnormal micturition. Her GP is treating her for acne.

85. A 21-year-old woman arrives in the Emergency Department with distorted facial expression and difficulty in speaking. She shows you a packet of tablets prescribed by her GP.

86. A 61-year-old man recently started on medication to control his blood pressure presents with a hot, swollen and painful right big toe.

Theme: Drug interactions

Options

A	Amoxicillin	F	Minocycline
B	Bumetanide	G	Protamine sulphate
C	Cefalexin	H	Spironolactone
D	Cimetidine	I	Streptokinase
E	Ciprofloxacin	J	Vitamin K

From the list above select the drug MOST LIKELY to be responsible for the adverse event described in the following cases. Each option may be used once, more than once, or not at all.

87. A 57-year-old chronic asthmatic on theophylline is treated for dysuria and frequency by her GP. She is brought into the Emergency Department with a pulseless ventricular tachycardia.

88. A 61-year-old man with a prosthetic heart valve is warfarinised. In hospital for an angiogram, his International normalised ratio (INR) is noted to be 6.9 and he has a severe nosebleed. The House Officer starts treatment without consulting his senior colleagues. Twelve hours later the patient has a new cardiac murmur and severe heart failure.

89. A 43-year-old man with a renal transplant is treated for a 'chest infection' by his GP. Three days later, after admission to hospital, he is noted to have severe renal failure.

90. A 67-year-old man on digoxin for atrial fibrillation is brought into the Emergency Department with severe muscular weakness. He has multiple ventricular ectopic beats and small T waves on the ECG.

91. A 64-year-old non-insulin-dependent diabetic, normally well controlled on metformin and diet, is brought into the Emergency Department unconscious. On testing, his bedside glucose reading (BM stix) is 2.0. He has recently started a new medicine prescribed by his GP.

Theme: Urea and electrolytes

Options

A	Na^+ 145 Ca^{2+} 2.3	K^+ 2.8 CK 39	Ur 4.0 Glu 4.7	Cr 88
B	Na^+ 141 Ca^{2+} 2.29	K^+ 3.9 CK 111	Ur 6.2 Glu 4.9	Cr 60
C	Na^+ 135 Ca^{2+} 2.28	K^+ 6.2 CK 122	Ur 6.1 Glu 5.1	Cr 71
D	Na^+ 142 Ca^{2+} 2.3	K^+ 6.4 CK 2210	Ur 16 Glu 4.5	Cr 158
E	Na^+ 154 Ca^{2+} 2.25	K^+ 5.9 CK 144	Ur 21 Glu 45	Cr 160
F	Na^+ 144 Ca^{2+} 2.04	K^+ 4.0 CK 123	Ur 24 Glu 14.5	Cr 110

Units: sodium (Na^+), mmol/l; potassium (K^+), mmol/l; urea (Ur), mmol/l; creatinine (Cr), mmol/l; calcium (Ca^{2+}), mmol/l; creatinine kinase (CK), U/l; glucose, mmol/l.

From the list above select the SINGLE most appropriate set of blood results to correspond with the cases described below. Each option may be used once, more than once, or not at all.

92. A 78-year-old woman who is taking an ACE inhibitor and spironolactone to treat her worsening congestive cardiac failure is brought in with palpitations and a low blood pressure.

93. An elderly man is brought to the Emergency Department by ambulance, having been found on the floor by his neighbour. He has been there all night, unable to get up.

94. A 23-year-old man has severe diarrhoea, having just returned from holiday. He is able to tolerate oral fluids.

95. A 23-year-old soldier who has been on a tough military exercise presents to the Emergency Department with discoloured urine.

96. A 51-year-old man presents with severe epigastric pain going through to his back. It is constant in nature and he had a similar episode one year ago. He is known to be a heavy drinker. His ECG is normal.

97. A 66-year-old obese man is brought into the Emergency Department semiconscious. His cleaner found him unwell in bed. He takes bendroflumethiazide (bendrofluazide) for his hypertension and had been out to dinner the night before. He has not vomited nor had diarrhoea.

Theme: Mental Health Act

Options

A	Common law	F	Section 4
B	No action	G	Section 5
C	Section 1	H	Section 12
D	Section 2	I	Section 136
E	Section 3	J	Section 458

From the list above select the SINGLE most appropriate course of action in response to the cases described below. Each option may be used once, more than once, or not at all.

98. A houseman is called to attend to an acutely disturbed elderly inpatient on a ward. The patient wishes to leave the hospital but clearly requires medical help.

99. An Emergency Department SHO is treating an acutely disturbed young man brought in by his friends from a nightclub. He has taken ecstasy for the first time.

100. An Emergency Department SHO is treating an anorexic 17-year-old girl weighing 38 kg who claims to have taken 28 paracetamol tablets approximately 12 hours ago with a bottle of wine. She appears under the influence of alcohol and now wishes to leave the department.

101. A police officer encounters a middle-aged man behaving in a very bizarre manner in the centre of a main road and thinks he has an acute mental disorder requiring treatment.

102. A middle-aged lady has taken 40 paracetamol tablets one hour ago. The Emergency Department SHO wishes to undertake a four-hour plasma paracetamol level and begin *N*-acetylcysteine if required. The patient wishes to leave the department. The SHO carefully explains that the patient might die of liver failure if she goes home. The woman appears highly intelligent, understands the situation and is deemed to be medically competent. She starts to leave.

Theme: Headache

Options

A	Bacterial meningitis	F	Cryptococcal meningitis
B	Basilar migraine	G	Herpes encephalitis
C	Benign intracranial hypertension	H	Normal-pressure hydrocephalus
D	Cerebrovascular accident	I	Transient ischaemic attack
E	Chronic subdural haematoma	J	Subarachnoid haemorrhage

Which of the causes of headache from the above list of options would be the MOST APPROPRIATE response for each of the situations given below? Each option may be used once, more than once, or not at all.

103. A 75-year-old woman is brought into the Emergency Department with a history of headache, forgetfulness and urinary incontinence for the preceding three weeks.

104. A 23-year-old man with mild headache, low-grade fever and malaise. He has been unwell for five days. On examination you notice facial molluscum contagiosum.

105. A 36-year-old man with sudden onset of the worst headache he has ever experienced. The pain is mostly occipital and he has a reduced Glasgow Coma Scale score.

106. A 19-year-old female university student has fever, headache and cervical rigidity.

107. A 28-year-old rugby player presents to the Emergency Department midway through the season with a two-week history of ataxia and difficulty passing urine.

108. An obese 29-year-old woman presents with a three-month history of recurrent headaches and associated visual disturbance. She is on the oral contraceptive pill and on examination she is noted to have papilloedema.

Theme: ECG

Options

- A Delta wave
- B Left axis deviation
- C Left bundle branch block
- D Mobitz type II second-degree heart block
- E Mobitz type I second-degree heart block
- F Prolonged QT interval
- G Reversed-tick-ST segment depression
- H Right axis deviation
- I Right bundle branch block
- J Saddle-shaped-ST segment elevation
- K ST-segment elevation
- L Third-degree atrioventricular block

From the above list of options select the SINGLE most appropriate ECG diagnosis in response to the cases described. Each option may be used once, more than once, or not at all.

109. A 74-year-old woman who has been accidentally taking too many digoxin tablets at home.

110. A 54-year-old man with repeating sequences of increasing PR interval followed by a dropped ventricular complex.

111. A 78-year-old man with known ischaemic heart disease is noted to have an rSR′ pattern in lead V_1.

112. A 59-year-old woman on high-dose chlorpromazine is treated for a chest infection with erythromycin. She develops torsades de pointes which is converted to sinus rhythm by cardioversion. A resting ECG is taken post-reversion to sinus rhythm.

113. A thin 20-year-old man has a QRS axis of +150°. He is otherwise well.

114. A 12-year-old boy under the care of the cardiologists for recurrent supraventricular tachycardias (SVTs) comes to the Emergency Department having had a 30-minute episode of palpitations with shortness of breath. These have resolved spontaneously and he is in sinus rhythm. His resting ECG is abnormal.

Theme: Acute hot knee

Options

- A Anterior cruciate ligament disruption
- B Baker's cyst
- C Gonococcal arthritis
- D Gout
- E Lyme arthritis
- F Pre-patellar bursitis
- G Pseudogout
- H Rheumatoid arthritis
- I Septic arthritis
- J Systemic lupus erythematosus (SLE)

Select the SINGLE most appropriate diagnosis in response to the cases described below from the above list of options. Each option may be used once, more than once, or not at all.

115. A 29-year-old woman with a swollen knee, pyrexia and an erythematous macular rash on her palms and soles of her feet.

116. A 55-year-old carpet layer with an acutely swollen knee. He is apyrexial and has a normal white cell count.

117. A 31-year-old woman with a hot swollen knee. She has a raised erythrocyte sedimentation rate (ESR) and raised C-reactive protein (CRP). She has felt generally unwell for a week.

118. A 67-year-old woman presents with a painful, hot, swollen knee. Her joint aspirate is turbid and shows positively birefringent rhomboid crystals on microscopy.

119. A 12-year-old boy with a hot swollen left knee, raised ESR, pyrexia and severe pain on passive movement. His joint aspirate is turbid.

Theme: Full blood count

Options

A	Hb 4.9	WCC 0.9	platelets 38
B	Hb 13.2	WCC 18.1	platelets 121
C	Hb 19.8	WCC 8.9	platelets 399
D	Hb 13.7	WCC 6.8	platelets 22
E	Hb 14.5	WCC 3.2	platelets 589

Units: haemoglobin (Hb), g/dl; white cell count (WCC), cells $\times 10^9$/l; platelets, cells $\times 10^9$/l

For each case select the SINGLE most appropriate set of blood results from the above list of options. Each option may be used once, more than once, or not at all.

120. A 67-year-old man presents with pain and swelling in his left lower leg. He has had several similar previous episodes that required treatment. He has a plethoric appearance and has severe itching after taking a bath. His spleen is mildly enlarged.

121. A 23-year-old pregnant woman is heparinised for a presumed pulmonary embolism. Six days later she remains fully well and a full blood count is taken.

122. A 35-year-old woman is diagnosed as hyperthyroid by her GP. He starts her on carbimazole. One week later she returns with a sore throat. The GP repeats her thyroid function tests and her full blood count.

123. A 27-year-old man falls from a roof and injures his abdomen. He requires splenectomy to arrest the bleeding. He recovers well post-operatively. Fourteen days later a full blood count is taken.

124. A 5-year-old boy is brought into hospital with a high fever and decreased level of consciousness. His mother tells you that he was mildly unwell with bright-red cheeks about ten days ago.

Theme: Advanced paediatric life support

Options

- A Approach patient with caution
- B Bedside blood glucose test (BM stix)
- C Bolus of intravenous fluids – 20 ml/kg
- D Chest compressions – 100/min
- E Chest drain insertion
- F Chin lift to open the airway
- G Dial emergency services from nearest phone
- H High-flow oxygen through a mask with reservoir bag
- I Jaw thrust to open airway with cervical spine control
- J Needle thoracocentesis
- K Two large intravenous cannulae
- L Two rescue breaths
- M Urgent cefotaxime intravenously

For each case below select the SINGLE most appropriate intervention from the above list of options. Each option may be used once, more than once, or not at all.

125. A 5-year-old boy has been hit by a car on a busy main road. He is prone and motionless. He does not appear to be breathing.

126. A 7-year-old girl is rushed into the Emergency Department by her parents. She is unconscious, very hot to touch and has a widespread purpuric rash. She is making loud grunting noises on expiration. Her breathing is shallow and rapid. Her pulse is barely palpable.

127. A 12-year-old boy was playing with petrol in a condemned house. He has severe burns to his face and neck and an obviously deformed ankle. There is no other history. He has spoken to the ambulance crew but his breathing is now beginning to deteriorate.

128. A 14-year-old boy has a single knife wound to the right side of the chest. He is sitting up and crying out with pain. He refuses an oxygen mask and his saturations are 93% on air and his respiratory rate is higher than expected. His trachea is central. His blood pressure, pulse and capillary refill are stable.

129. A 4-year-old girl with congenital heart disease has a cardiac arrest in her bed on the paediatric ward. You are the first person to arrive. The child is unresponsive.

130. A 6-year-old girl arrives in the Emergency Department with severe asthma. She can barely talk and has a very high respiratory rate with use of accessory muscles and visible intercostal recession. Her pulse rate is 140 bpm.

Theme: Chest pain

Options

A	Coronary artery spasm	G	Pericarditis
B	Dissection of thoracic aorta	H	Pneumonia
C	Gastro-oesophageal reflux disease	I	Pneumothorax
		J	Pulmonary embolism
D	Mesothelioma	K	Tietze's disease
E	Metastatic lung deposits	L	Unstable angina
F	Oesophageal spasm		

From each case below select the SINGLE most appropriate diagnosis from the above list of options. Each option may be used once, more than once, or not at all.

131. A 25-year-old man with central chest pain, tachycardia and sweating. He has taken cocaine.

132. A 63-year-old male smoker with long-term hypertension. He has severe chest pain radiating through to his back.

133. A 37-year-old lady with severe left-sided pain, which is worse on inspiration. She has antiphospholipid syndrome and a swollen left ankle.

134. A 42-year-old man with central chest pain. Movement exacerbates the pain and the anterior chest wall is tender.

135. A 67-year-old male industrial worker with left-sided chest pain and long-term pleural plaques.

136. An obese 42-year-old lady with central chest pain going through to her back, which is partially alleviated by sitting forward.

Theme: Asthma

Options

A Acute severe asthma
B Arterial blood gas analysis
C Chest X-ray
D Intravenous hydrocortisone
E Intravenous magnesium
F Intravenous salbutamol
G Intubation and ventilation
H Life-threatening asthma
I Moderate asthma
J Near-fatal asthma
K Nebulised salbutamol and ipratropium bromide
L Oral prednisolone

For each question below select the SINGLE most appropriate response from the above list of options. Each option may be used once, more than once, or not at all.

137. A 23-year-old man presents to the Emergency Department with an acute asthma attack and a peak expiratory flow reading 55% of predicted. How is his asthma classified?

138. A 19-year-old girl has an acute severe asthma attack and it fails to respond to initial nebulised therapy in the Emergency Department. Her oxygen saturations are deteriorating. What is the next step?

139. A 45-year-old woman is rushed into the Emergency Department. She meets the criteria for a diagnosis of near-fatal asthma. She is sitting upright and fighting for breath, with an oxygen mask and reservoir bag. What is her initial management?

140. A 37-year-old man has the following blood gas analysis: Po_2 7.9 kPa, Pco_2 4.41 kPa and oxygen saturations of 87%. How is his asthma classified?

141. A 21-year-old man has an acute asthma attack. He is hypoxic and has a raised Pco_2. What does definitive management require?

Theme: Red blood cells

Options

- A Fragment cells
- B Hypochromia, anisocytosis, poikilocytosis
- C Pancytopenia with hypocellular bone marrow
- D Pancytopenia with normal bone marrow function
- E Raised mean corpuscular volume (MCV) with macrocytosis and normal bone marrow
- F Raised MCV with megaloblasts in bone marrow
- G Raised red cell count and bone marrow erythroid hyperplasia
- H Sickle cells
- I Sideroblasts, basophilic stippling
- J Spherocytes and reticulocytes

Which one of the above sets of blood/bone-marrow results would represent the most likely findings for each of the situations below. Each option may be used once, more than once, or not at all.

142. A 56-year-old man with pernicious anaemia.

143. A 63-year-old man with a prosthetic heart valve.

144. A 23-year-old man has previously been admitted for recurrent chest pains and now presents with priapism.

145. A 45-year-old lady with rheumatoid arthritis and a large spleen.

146. A 9-year-old boy with lead poisoning.

147. A 31-year-old Tanzanian man with hookworm infection.

Theme: Management of cardiac arrest

Options

A	Bag-valve-mask ventilation	G	Insert a chest drain
B	Defibrillate at 100 J	H	Intravenous adrenaline
C	Defibrillate at 200 J	I	Intravenous atropine
D	Defibrillate at 360 J	J	Needle thoracocentesis
E	Endotracheal intubation	K	Precordial thump
F	External cardiac massage	L	Synchronised cardioversion

For each scenario described below, choose the SINGLE most appropriate treatment from the above list of options. Each option may be used once, more than once, or not at all.

148. A 56-year-old man is brought to the Emergency Department with a regular, broad-complex tachycardia at a rate of 130/minute on the ECG monitor. He is not breathing and has no palpable central pulse.

149. A 23-year-old man has been stabbed in the right chest. Cardiopulmonary resuscitation (CPR) is in progress and he has been intubated. You diagnose pulseless electrical activity (PEA).

150. On the Coronary Care Unit ward round a 73-year-old patient suddenly stops talking and you notice ventricular fibrillation (VF) on the cardiac monitor. He has a drip in his left arm.

151. A 17-year-old girl has been brought from a fire in a caravan by her family. In the Emergency Department she is asystolic. The ambulance crew have started bag-mask ventilation and chest compressions and just given adrenaline (epinephrine).

152. A 35-week-pregnant lady is brought to the Emergency Department by the paramedics. They have managed to intubate and start CPR. She has no palpable pulse and a flat line on the ECG monitor.

153. A 64-year-old man is intubated and ventilated after a cardiac arrest. His initial rhythm in hospital is VF. After one shock, the rhythm is asytole on the monitor.

154. After a VF arrest, a 73-year-old man has a central pulse and is in sinus rhythm. He had six shocks in total; the last shock was 360 J. A few minutes later he deteriorates back into VF.

Theme: Basic life support management

Options

A	Check airway	E	Leave patient
B	Check pulse	F	No action
C	Continue CPR until exhausted	G	Place in recovery position
D	Give rescue breaths	H	Start chest compressions

For each patient described below, choose the SINGLE most appropriate treatment from the above list of options. Each option may be used once, more than once, or not at all.

155. A 6-year-old has stopped breathing in the supermarket. You have given mouth-to-mouth ventilation. What do you do next?

156. A 73-year-old visitor collapses in the hospital shop. You are alone. You open his airway and find he is not breathing.

157. A 43-year-old man collapses in the street. After two rescue breaths he starts groaning.

158. A ventilated patient on the Intensive Care Unit becomes asystolic despite good progress noticed on the ward round only 30 minutes earlier.

159. You rescue a 17-year-old boy from under the water in a canal. He is in cardiac arrest. You perform cardiopulmonary resuscitation alone for one minute and stop to assess your next action. The patient is unresponsive and cold.

160. There has been a bomb in the underground train station and the man in the seat next to you has stopped breathing. Your train is full of black smoke and you can see a fire.

Theme: Management of poisoning

Options

A	Adrenaline (epinephrine)	F	Glucose
B	Calcium	G	Isoprenaline
C	Dobutamine	H	Naloxone
D	Flumazenil	I	None of the above
E	Glucagon		

For each patient described below, choose the SINGLE most appropriate treatment from the above list of options. Each option may be used once, more than once, or not at all.

161. A 23-year-old rugby player has had his dislocated shoulder reduced using Entonox and midazolam. His conscious level decreases and he has falling oxygen saturations despite high-flow oxygen.

162. An 83-year-old lady on the ward has recently had a total hip replacement. She has become very drowsy, with small pupils and a respiratory rate of 8/minute.

163. A patient has taken an overdose and is brought into the Emergency Department. He has a Glasgow Coma Scale (GCS) score of 6. The patient's partner reports that the patient has taken diazepam and amitriptyline.

164. A 17-year-old girl has been found drowsy at school. She has a GCS score of 12. You are unable to gain venous access but her capillary blood sugar is 2.1.

165. A 23-year-old man has taken an atenolol overdose with alcohol. He has been intubated and ventilated however, his blood pressure is 70/30 mmHg despite fluid replacement and atropine.

Theme: Child with a painful leg

Options

A	Fractured femur	F	Perthes disease
B	Irritable hip	G	Septic arthritis
C	Non-accidental injury	H	Shin splints
D	Osgood–Schlatter disease	I	Sickle cell disease
E	Osteomyelitis	J	Slipped femoral epiphysis

For each patient described below, choose the SINGLE most likely diagnosis from the above list of options. Each option may be used once, more than once, or not at all.

166. A 5-year-old boy has a painful limp for a few weeks. Examination reveals limited movement at the hip. X-ray of the hip shows sclerosis of the femoral head. The parents deny any trauma.

167. A 13-year-old boy who is overweight develops hip pain after a minor fall. An X-ray of the hip is abnormal.

168. A 12-year-old child who enjoys sports develops a tender tibial tuberosity.

169. A 6-year-old boy develops a limp after an upper respiratory tract infection. X-rays are normal.

170. A 5-month-old girl is brought in to the Emergency Department by her nanny because she has been crying all morning. Her left thigh is swollen. There is no history of trauma.

Theme: Blood gas analysis

Options

A	Diabetes	E	Primary hyperventilation
B	Head injury	F	Pulmonary embolism
C	Mild asthma	G	Severe asthma
D	Paracetamol poisoning	H	Tension pneumothorax

For each of the following blood gas results, select the SINGLE most likely diagnosis from the above list of options. Each option may be used once, more than once, or not at all.

171.	pH 6.91	P_{CO_2} 2.6	P_{O_2} 15.7	Base excess –22
172.	pH 7.52	P_{CO_2} 2.6	P_{O_2} 15.7	Base excess +2
173.	pH 7.37	P_{CO_2} 2.6	P_{O_2} 9.4	Base excess +2
174.	pH 7.21	P_{CO_2} 7.4	P_{O_2} 8.4	Base excess +8

Units: P_{CO_2}, kPa; P_{O_2}, kPa; base excess, mmol/l.

Theme: Management of common injuries in the Emergency Department

Options

A	Initial management of injury followed by X-ray	C	X-ray before management but no further X-ray
B	No X-ray needed in the Emergency Department	D	X-ray before management then a check X-ray

For each patient described below choose the SINGLE most appropriate action from the above list of options. Each option may be used once, more than once, or not at all.

175. The patient has obvious deformity to the shoulder with loss of deltoid contour after a motorcycle accident; no other injury.

176. Clinical anterior dislocation of the right shoulder for the fourth time when the patient raised her arms.

177. A pedestrian is hit by a car, his foot is twisted to the side. You suspect a fracture dislocation.

178. Dislocated mandible after a patient yawned.

179. An obvious deformity to the nose after a fall.

180. A plant pot is dropped on a foot, making the second toe very tender and swollen but with no angulation.

Theme: Management of pneumothorax

Options

A	Chest drain in fifth intercostal space, mid-axillary line	D	Needle aspiration
B	Chest drain in second intercostal space, mid-clavicular line	E	No intervention except regular X-ray
C	Immediate needle thoracocentesis	F	Referral to cardiothoracic surgeons

For each of the situations described below choose the SINGLE most appropriate treatment from the above list of options. Each option may be used once, more than once, or not at all.

181. A 29-year-old man with no lung disease develops a spontaneous pneumothorax. X-ray shows complete collapse but no evidence of tension.

182. A 14-year-old boy has been hit by a car and has decreased air entry into the left chest with a resonant percussion note and evidence of mediastinal shift to the right.

183. A 28-year-old man has been stabbed in the right chest. He is mildly breathless and has evidence of a simple pneumothorax.

184. A 32-year-old woman has a large spontaneous pneumothorax. Five litres of air are aspirated but the check X-ray is unchanged.

185. A 72-year-old man has been impaled by a spike through his right chest. He removed the spike but now has a hole in his chest wall through which air is seen to pass.

186. A 24-year-old thin man develops a small spontaneous pneumothorax. He is in pain but is not breathless.

Theme: Diagnosis of rashes

Options

A	Behçet's syndrome	F	Pityriasis rosea
B	Contact dermatitis	G	Pityriasis versicolor
C	Dermatitis herpetiformis	H	Psoriasis
D	Eczema	I	Scabies
E	Lichen planus	J	Vitiligo

For each description choose the SINGLE most likely diagnosis from the above list of options. Each option may be used once, more than once, or not at all.

187. Very itchy, flat-topped papule on the flexor surface of the wrist with white lesions in the mouth.

188. Pink oval macules on the trunk with peripheral scaling, preceded by a larger patch the week before.

189. Depigmented patches on the trunk with fine scale that have appeared in a Caucasian patient after a holiday in the sun.

190. Red scaly plaques on the knees.

191. Itchy small blisters on the shoulders that have been scratched to cause raw areas. The patient has coeliac disease.

Theme: Causes of a non-blanching rash

Options

A	Acute leukaemia	E	Henoch–Schönlein purpura
B	Cushing's disease	F	Immune thrombocytopenic purpura
C	Fat embolism syndrome	G	Meningococcal septicaemia
D	Haemolytic-uraemic syndrome	H	Non-accidental injury

For the following descriptions choose the SINGLE most likely diagnosis from the above list of options. Each option may be used once, more than once, or not at all.

192. A child with malaise and a mild fever presents with a purpuric rash on the buttocks and legs. Otherwise he is well.

193. Following a recent upper respiratory tract infection, a previously well child has started to bruise easily. Initial blood tests are normal apart from a very low platelet count.

194. A child presents with four lines of purpura along the outer thigh. He has a normal platelet count.

195. A very sick child with high fever, a purpuric rash on the limbs and a prolonged capillary refill time.

196. A 6-year-old child has developed widespread petechiae and is pale. She has been unwell for a few weeks with recurrent infections.

Theme: Endocrine disease

Options

A	Addison's disease	F	Multiple endocrine neoplasia
B	Conn's syndrome	G	Phaeochromocytoma
C	Cushing's syndrome	H	Syndrome of inappropriate antidiuretic hormone secretion
D	Diabetes insipidus		
E	Graves' disease		

From the following scenarios choose the SINGLE most likely diagnosis from the above list of options. Each option may be used once, more than once, or not at all.

197. A 56-year-old woman presents to the Emergency Department with syncope. You notice she has a significant postural drop in blood pressure and also pigmentation in a recent scar on her neck.

198. A 48-year-old lady has developed striae on her abdomen and is hypertensive.

199. A 31-year-old woman has severe hypertension and is found to have a potassium level of 3.1 mmol/l.

200. A 32-year-old woman has a history of episodes of severe headache and anxiety with flushing. On examination she is very hypertensive and tachycardic.

EMQ PRACTICE EXAMINATION – ANSWERS AND EXPLANATIONS

Theme: Upper abdominal pain

1. G

Gallstones are infrequently visible on X-ray but are the commonest cause of acute pancreatitis in the UK. Pancreatitis is also associated with acute and chronic alcohol use, mumps, trauma and can be seen post-operatively in upper abdominal surgery. The diagnosis is usually made on the history and the presence of a very elevated serum amylase.

2. F

The high JVP indicates right-sided heart failure. Myocardial infarction is an important cause of epigastric pain and an electrocardiogram (ECG) should always be performed.

3. H

The assessment of patients with other serious disease can be very difficult. This man has recently received methylprednisolone and is at increased risk of upper gastrointestinal (GI) bleeding or perforation. The presence of a rigid abdomen and no bowel sounds should always raise the suspicion of bowel perforation. This man is unable to have an erect chest X-ray and a left lateral decubitus film is used to demonstrate free gas. The film is taken after the patient has been lying on his left side for 15–20 minutes. The film is taken with a horizontal beam and any free gas will be seen above the liver to give a long dark shadow.

4. B

Intermittent epigastric symptoms with a tender right upper quadrant are associated with biliary colic. If associated with jaundice, urgent investigation by ultrasound scan is required to exclude a gallstone in the common bile duct as there is a risk of ascending cholangitis. Acute cholecystitis may occur on a background history of biliary colic but with a presentation including fever, occasionally with rigors, severe right upper quadrant pain and a positive Murphy's sign.

5. A

This man is taking non-steroidal anti-inflammatory drugs (NSAIDS) for his arthritis. Gastrointestinal bleeding is a frequent cause of collapse in the elderly. The hypovolaemia is demonstrated by the postural drop in blood pressure. He is not tachycardic because he is using β-blockers for his hypertension.

Theme: Painful upper limb

6. G

With a scaphoid fracture there is pain on abducting the thumb. The tenderness is in the anatomical snuffbox area (bordered by the tendons of extensor pollicis longus on the ulnar side and extensor pollicis brevis and abductor pollicis brevis on the radial side) as well as in the thenar eminence. Gamekeeper's thumb is disruption of the ulnar collateral ligament of the thumb at the metacarpophalangeal joint with tenderness at this level.

7. H

This is an orthopaedic emergency. In a fracture of the supracondylar region of the humerus the triceps pulls the forearm posteriorly, resulting in impingement of the brachial artery on the fracture end. The resultant pressure puts the vascular supply to the forearm at risk, hence the poorly palpable radial artery.

8. F

Electric shock and epilepsy are two of the commonest associations with posterior dislocation of the shoulder.

9. D

In older patients a fracture of the shaft of the humerus is also possible and can be associated with radial nerve palsy due to injury to the nerve as it passes down the spiral groove. Falls in women of this age may also result in a Colles' fracture of the forearm.

10. B

De Quervain's tenosynovitis occurs as a result of repetitive movements such as may be encountered in factory work. Pain is often worse at night. The swelling is of the sheath around the abductor pollicis longus and extensor pollicis brevis tendons at the radial styloid.

Theme: Carcinogenesis

11. **B**

12. **H**

13. **C**

14. **E**

These tumours may constitute occupational diseases if the exposure was in the course of work in a recognised industry. This may enable the individual to claim compensation for their disease.

15. **G**

Oestrogens are associated with vaginal and endometrial carcinoma.

Aflatoxins are associated with hepatocellular carcinoma. Epstein–Barr virus is associated with Burkitt's lymphoma.

Theme: Causes of collapse in a woman who is 35 weeks' pregnant

16. C

Aortocaval compression occurs earlier in the pregnancies of multiparous women. Symptoms often occur when recumbent but for multiparous women or in multiple pregnancies the symptoms can develop when seated during the day.

17. D

Eclampsia is more common in first pregnancies and in women who had eclampsia or pre-eclampsia in their first pregnancy. The symptoms and signs of pre-eclampsia are proteinuria, headache, oedema, hypertension and visual disturbance, which may be picked up in antenatal screening if attended. Eclampsia is said to exist once the patient has fitted; prior to this the diagnosis is pre-eclampsia.

18. G

The signs are of septicaemia. It is likely that the watery discharge is due to premature rupture of membranes causing a slow leak of liquor and resulting in ascending infection.

19. E

Collapse and severe abdominal pain indicates uterine catastrophe. Placental abruption may be concealed, with no vaginal bleeding. The uterus is hard. There is a very high risk of fetal death and an absent fetal heart may be apparent on presentation. Placental abruption may follow trauma and is more common with severe hypertension.

20. A

Amniotic fluid embolism occurs in labour, usually at the height of a contraction. The presentation is that of shock with cyanosis. The central venous pressure (CVP) is raised. Associated factors are the presence of a uterine scar, polyhydramnios and the use of syntocinon. Chest X-ray shows mottled opacities and it is usually fatal. Post-mortem examination reveals widespread disseminated intravascular coagulation.

Theme: Biochemistry of jaundice

21. C

In Gilbert's syndrome the bilirubin is unconjugated due to congenital failure of the hepatocyte to take up the bilirubin for conjugation. There is no bilirubin in the urine as only the conjugated form is water-soluble and appears in the urine. Dubin–Johnson syndrome is the congenital failure of excretion of the conjugated bilirubin into the bile canaliculi.

22. B

The very elevated alkaline phosphatase in the presence of jaundice indicates extrahepatic obstruction, typically from a common bile duct stone or carcinoma of the head of the pancreas.

23. E

In intrahepatic cholestasis the AST is very elevated but the alkaline phosphatase, which arises form the bile duct walls, is not. Common causes are drugs, alcohol and infective hepatitis.

24. D

In haemolytic jaundice there will be anaemia. There is no elevation in urinary bilirubin because the haemolysis releases unconjugated bilirubin which is not water-soluble and therefore will not appear in the urine.

Theme: Death in hospital

25. C

Only a qualified doctor can certify death. A senior nurse, appropriately trained, can verify death. Neither a medical student nor a paramedic can certify death. Some paramedics are now trained to verify death in the pre-hospital environment in very specific clinical conditions such as decomposition of the body, severed head, etc.

26. B

An appropriately trained senior nurse can verify death and the body can be moved to the mortuary for later certification by a doctor in most hospitals.

27. E

All deaths within 30 days of surgery must be reported to the Coroner. Unless the Coroner decides otherwise, he or she will be responsible for issuing the death certificate.

28. G

As the patient has not been under your care for more than 24 hours you are not able to issue a death certificate. This case should be referred to the Coroner, but given the history, if the GP has seen the patient within 14 days of his death, the GP can issue the death certificate.

29. E

The cause of death would seem to be unrelated to the relatively minor trauma but all trauma-related deaths must be referred to the Coroner, as must deaths thought to be due to privation or neglect.

Theme: Vaginal bleeding

30. D

This woman gives a history consistent with pregnancy. The open os and low abdominal pain associated with heavy vaginal bleeding indicate inevitable abortion.

31. A

The recurrence of abnormal vaginal bleeding in a patient with a previous history of a cone biopsy would raise concerns of carcinoma of the cervix. Her last smear was nearly five years ago, indicating she defaulted from follow-up after her cone biopsy. Six weeks' amenorrhoea might raise concerns about an ectopic pregnancy but the absence of pain makes this unlikely. It would always be wise to perform a pregnancy test and scan if in any doubt.

32. G

This woman has been investigated for peri-menopausal bleeding. Investigations for both cervical and endometrial carcinoma are negative. Only once these causes have been excluded can this be confirmed as normal menstruation.

33. I

Menorrhagia is excessive bleeding that might be manifest as either heavy or prolonged periods. The most likely cause in this age range is uterine fibroids. The uterus is often bulky. Ultrasound scan can confirm the diagnosis.

34. H

This pregnant woman has light vaginal blood loss with no abdominal pain and a closed cervical os on examination. In threatened abortion an early ultrasound scan is essential to confirm a viable intrauterine pregnancy. This could be a missed abortion if the ultrasound is incompatible with dates and fails to demonstrate a viable fetus.

Theme: Sexually transmitted diseases

35. I

A common cause of vaginal discharge, caused by the flagellate protozoan, *Trichomonas*. It causes a profuse greenish discharge.

36. G

Primary syphilis presents as a papule in the mucosa of the lower genital tract, mouth or anorectal region. After one week it becomes a chancre – a single painless indurated ulcer. Dark-field examination of a smear from the ulcer base demonstrated *Treponema pallidum*.

37. F

Lymphogranuloma venereum is caused by *Chlamydia trachomatis* serotypes L1, L2 and L3. Other serotypes cause a superficial inflammation of the mucosa and are associated with infertility. The classic finding is of matted inguinal lymph nodes with abscess and sinus formation. The primary lesion is a small papule in the lower genital tract which breaks down to form a painless ulcer.

38. D

Herpes simplex is a sexually transmitted disease caused by either herpes simplex virus 1 or 2. The lesions are typical small clusters of vesicles but in the moist environment of the vulva they will often appear as small extremely painful ulcers, which can precipitate urinary retention secondary to pain.

39. C

The commonest sexually transmitted disease causing a milky urethral discharge in men is gonorrhoea. Up to 50% of men and women with gonorrhoea are asymptomatic.

Theme: Discoloured urine

40. H

Rifampicin is used for prophylaxis in cases of close contact with meningococcal disease. It results in red discoloration of urine and tears, hence the pink contact lenses. Patients should be counselled about this side-effect and should be advised not to use contact lenses as the staining may be permanent.

41. E

Dark urine and pale stools are indicative of cholestasis. Haemolysis will result in urine which turns dark on standing, due to urobilinogen, but the stools will remain a normal colour and there will be no steatorrhoea. In pancreatic carcinoma there will be extrahepatic cholestasis and steatorrhoea, resulting in faeces which float due to their fat content and are difficult to flush away.

42. D

Myoglobinuria may occur with hyperpyrexia and the physical exertion at a rave, particularly associated with the ingestion of ecstasy (methylenedioxymethamfetamine MDMA).

43. J

A urethral tumour will result in blood in the initial stream of urine. The patient should have a dipstick examination of an initial stream of urine and urethroscopy.

44. F

The commonest form of porphyria seen in the UK is acute intermittent porphyria. The disease has an autosomal dominant inheritance and may be precipitated by drugs, including barbiturates, sulphonamides, griseofulvin and the oral contraceptive pill. The urine has excess porphobilinogen during an attack, which will darken the urine on standing due to oxidation.

Theme: Urgent investigations of emergency presentations

45. I

The diagnosis to be excluded by initial ultrasound examination is that of a testicular tumour. The initial presentation will often be following minor trauma resulting in some discomfort and self-examination, which brings the patient to the doctor. No scrotal lesion which may be a tumour should be biopsied due to the high risk of implantation with a consequent poorer prognosis. The history of orchidopexy indicates a higher risk of testicular tumour.

46. B

The symptoms and signs indicate the posterior fossa being the likely site of a tumour. Posterior fossa tumours are more common in children, with a medulloblastoma of the cerebellum being the commonest. In childhood the tumours are mainly in the midline. A CT scan of the posterior fossa may miss a small tumour, especially in a child, so an MRI scan is the investigation of choice.

47. I

The clinical description is of right-sided peritonitis (rebound tenderness). In this situation, the most likely diagnosis would be appendicitis but there is a strong possibility of ectopic pregnancy or ovarian pathology. The urinary pregnancy test would almost always be positive in an ectopic pregnancy; a serum pregnancy test would take too long in most hospitals. The investigation of choice of those outlined would be an ultrasound scan. An alternative would be an on-table laparoscopy with both general surgeons and gynaecologists present.

48. G

Spiral CT scan. 'Collapse ?cause' is a common diagnostic dilemma in the Emergency Department. This man has a tachycardia, increased respiratory rate and right axis deviation on ECG. All of these indicate that a pulmonary embolus must be excluded. Spiral CT scan is the investigation of choice. A Technetium-99m scan can be used, but for diagnostic accuracy it must include a ventilation scan. Echocardiography can be used but only gives good diagnostic accuracy if performed by the transoesophageal route.

49. B

This woman has malignant cord compression. She is on tamoxifen for breast cancer, which has metastasised to the thoracic vertebrae. She has been taking paracetamol for bone pain. The classic symptoms are of weak legs and difficulty passing urine, leading on to incontinence. The investigaton of choice is an MRI scan to demonstrate the site and extent of the compression.

Theme: Rheumatology

50. H

Rheumatiod arthritis is more common in women than men. Swan-neck deformity and boutonnière deformity of the fingers are characteristic of the condition as is ulnar deviation of the fingers at the metacarpophalangeal joints. The distal interphalangeal joints are usually spared. Radiologically, erosions are the characteristic bone change, along with joint-space narrowing and osteoporosis. Bone destruction is a late finding.

51. J

Systemic lupus erythematosus (SLE) is nine times more common in women than men. It begins in young adulthood and is more common is those of African and Polynesian descent. The classic rash is a butterfly erthematous facial rash. Joint pain is commonly a prominent feature although examination is usually normal. Serum antinuclear antibodies are positive in almost all cases. Double-stranded DNA antibodies are specific but are seen in only 50% of cases.

52. C

Osteoarthritis is a degenerative arthritis affecting the large joints of the lower limbs in particular. The hand and finger joints (especially the distal interphalangeal joints) may be affected, including the carpometacarpal joint of the thumb. Crepitus is a common finding and is usually painless. Radiologically there is narrowing of the joint space and characteristic osteophyte formation.

53. A

Ankylosing spondylitis is a condition that becomes clinically apparent in late adolescence to early adulthood. It is more common in men than women. Susceptibility is related to HLA-B27 type. Radiologically, an early sign is erosion and sclerosis of the sacroiliac joints, accounting for the back pain.

54. E

Polymyalgia rheumatica occurs in patients over 60 years old, predominantly women. It presents with shoulder girdle pain, stiffness, and only very occasionally any weakness. Polymyositis presents with proximal muscle weakness. Polymyalgia rheumatica is associated with temporal arteritis, which may result in sudden visual loss. Treatment in this case is urgent high-dose steroids to relieve symptoms and prevent blindness in the other eye.

Theme: Shock

55. D

This man presents in shock following a history of trauma and with signs of a possible abdominal injury. The commonest cause of shock after trauma is haemorrhagic. Note his relatively high diastolic pressure which reflects the increased peripheral vascular resistance in response to blood loss.

56. E

This woman presents in shock following trauma. The commonest cause would be haemorrhagic shock but she has warm peripheries and a low diastolic pressure due to loss of peripheral vascular resistance, and a bradycardia due to the unopposed vagal effect on the heart seen with a high thoracic or cervical spinal injury causing neurogenic shock. This may obviously also be associated with blood loss, so initial management is to provide fluid replacement and to search for a cause of blood loss as well as investigation of the cause of neurogenic shock.

57. F

The presence of warm peripheries and a low diastolic blood pressure indicates the vasodilatation seen in septic shock. She is tachycardic which differentiates the diagnosis from neurogenic shock. The elderly and the very young may present in septic shock without a fever.

58. H

This man has suddenly deteriorated after the insertion of a CVP line, which has caused a tension pneumothorax. He has distended neck veins, indicating high intrathoracic pressure. Cardiac tamponade is possible based on the signs given but is less likely after insertion of a CVP line than is a pneumothorax.

59. C

This man has had an inferior myocardial infarction with an associated bradycardia and right heart failure, leading to cardiogenic shock.

Theme: Facial pain

60. D

Ludwig's angina results in symmetrical swelling of the floor of the mouth and upper neck due to dental infection.

61. I

Trigeminal neuralgia is a severe sudden pain in the distribution of the trigeminal nerve, which may be triggered by touch. It is more common in multiple sclerosis, when it may be bilateral.

62. G

In most parotid swellings the facial nerve is intact. Involvement of the facial nerve is associated with malignant tumours.

63. A

The association with increased pain on leaning forwards is seen in frontal sinusitis. Herpes zoster (shingles) can affect the frontal branch of the trigeminal nerve with pain before a rash is present, but this will not be worse on leaning forwards.

64. H

With a salivary duct stone, the swelling occurs in response to an increased flow of saliva when eating a meal.

Theme: Acute red eye

65. C

In viral conjunctivits infection produces a watery discharge with tarsal follicles.

66. G

The cornea is an avascular, transparent structure. A breach in the corneal epithelium is necessary for infection to become established. Bacterial infection is associated with a mucopurulent discharge. A hypopyon is seen when pus cells accumulate in the anterior chamber of the eye. The white opacity is the corneal ulcer. The most important viral keratitis is herpetic, with the formation of a dendritic ulcer which can usually only be seen after fluorescein staining.

67. F

This is acute iritis: the inflammation predominantly involves the iris and ciliary body. The pupil is smaller than the unaffected side. A hypopyon may be seen in severe cases when keratic precipitates (aggregates of cells on the posterior surface of the cornea) will be visible on slit lamp examination.

68. A

The main features of acute glaucoma are decreased vision associated with severe pain and constitutional upset. This condition is most commonly seen in older patients with long-sightedness. It is extremely important to ensure intraocular pressures are measured and pupil-constricting drops given to open up the angle, as well as drugs to reduce the production of aqueous humour, such as acetazolamide.

69. E

Episcleritis is unilateral and frequently recurrent. It is more common in women aged 30–40 years. The redness is confined to one quadrant of the eye. A tender nodule may be present at the centre of the inflamed area. It may be associated with connective tissue disorders.

Theme: Post-traumatic pain relief

70. G

The Glasgow Coma Scale score indicates a potential head injury and so, unless essential, opioids should be avoided.

71. D

The ankle injury described is unlikely to be a fracture. In pregnancy the first-line treatment for minor traumatic pain is paracetamol if a drug is needed. For severe pain it is safe to use opioids, especially in later pregnancy. Do not forget the joint reduction or fracture immobilisation is an effective means of pain relief in many cases and avoids the need for drugs.

72. I

You are unable to give opioids here. Skin traction provides good pain relief although you are likely to need some analgesia for the skin traction to be applied. Entonox may be used. Intramuscular analgesia is unreliable and in the elderly you should avoid NSAIDs because of the risk of renal failure.

73. E

This is the best analgesia in the absence of contraindications.

74. A

This man has compartment syndrome. This is most common in fractures of the forearm and lower leg. The presence of pulses does not exclude compartment syndrome. Persisting pain despite appropriate analgesia and fracture immobilisation raises the possibility of compartment syndrome. Pain out of proportion to clinical signs should always raise the possibility of an ischaemic cause.

Theme: Head injury

75. H

This is a fracture through the floor of the anterior cranial fossa, leading to 'panda eyes' (bruising not extending beyond the orbital margin) and cerebrospinal fluid (CSF) rhinorrhoea (mixed with blood). CSF rhinorrhoea may be diagnosed by the use of blotting paper (or hospital linen) which leaves a central blood clot surrounded by a stain of straw-coloured fluid, the CSF. A skull X-ray will often not reveal the fracture. Look for the sign of a fluid level in the sphenoidal sinus on the lateral skull X-ray.

76. B

The ellipse shape is due to bleeding into the subdural space. Subdural haematoma is associated with significant primary brain injury and associated cerebral swelling contributing to the midline shift and failure to regain consciousness after the initial injury. Treatment is urgent surgical removal of the haematoma and aggressive management of the cerebral oedema. Mortality is high (50–60%).

77. F

Three-month-old babies cannot roll over and would not be able to propel themselves off the changing table. Head injury in a child under the age of one year should always raise the suspicion of non-accidental injury.

78. A

You should not waste time getting a skull X-ray but proceed straight to CT scan. His history is of a brief period of loss of consciousness followed by a lucid interval and subsequent deterioration in conscious level. CT scan will show a lens-shaped (biconvex) appearance of the extradural haematoma. With urgent surgical evacuation, mortality is low (1–9%), reflecting the mild primary brain injury.

79. G

The CT scan description of blood in the basal cisterns (around the brainstem and midbrain) indicates subarachnoid haemorrhage (SAH). It is likely that this is not primarily traumatic, as he had pulled off the road prior to the accident. Traumatic SAH is not common. The presence of SAH following head injury should always raise the possibility that the SAH occurred first and resulted in the events which led to the head injury. Investigations should include identifying a berry aneurysm or other cause if present.

Theme: Drug side-effects

80. B

This patient has glandular fever (infectious mononucleosis) and has been treated for an upper respiratory tract infection by her GP. The combination of glandular fever and amoxicillin commonly produces a widespread erythematous rash. Amoxicillin can also cause rashes through a fixed drug reaction-type process, and a diffuse erythematous blanching rash with weals in the event of a severe sensitivity reaction.

81. D

This patient has been started on an angiotensin-converting enzyme (ACE) inhibitor for treatment of his hypertension. ACE inhibitors may cause profound hypotension when started. They should be initiated at a low dose and titrated upwards depending on blood pressure reduction and the patient's ability to tolerate the drug. ACE inhibitors may also cause severe cough in patients, requiring withdrawal of the medication.

82. K

This patient has tuberculosis requiring medical therapy. Red discoloration of urine is a frequent side-effect of the drug. It also causes deranged liver function tests, hepatitis and erythema nodosum. Rifampicin also induces the P450 enzyme system that in turn increases the rate of metabolism of oral contraceptives, sulphonylureas, ciclosporin and warfarin.

83. L

Protease inhibitors are an integral part of antiretroviral therapy. This is a rapidly developing area with high levels of research investment, but usually at least three drugs, including a protease inhibitor, are required for viral suppression to undetectable levels. Protease inhibitors have numerous side-effects, including pancreatitis (as above), abdominal pain, fat redistribution, blood disorders (anaemia, neutropenia, thrombocytopenia) and metabolic effects (hyper-lipidaemia, insulin resistance and hyperglycaemia).

84. J

This girl has developed benign intracranial hypertension secondary to the tetracycline therapy. Tetracyclines may also cause liver toxicity, photosensitivity and hypersensitivity reactions.

85. I

This patient has acute facial dystonia as a side-effect of the metoclopramide treatment. This uncommon reaction is well documented with the antidopaminergic antiemetics and should be treated with benzatropine (anticholinergic effect) or similar.

86. C

This patient is taking a thiazide diuretic for his hypertension and has acute gout. Thiazide diuretics are the first-line treatment for raised blood pressure but they cause raised urate levels, which may precipitate gout in some individuals. Thiazides also cause hypokalaemia, hyponatraemia, hypercalcaemia and hyperglycaemia.

Theme: Drug interactions

87. E

Ciprofloxacin increases the plasma levels of theophylline, leading to an increased risk of cardiac arrhythmias. If the two drugs are to be used together, the theophylline dose should be reduced and the plasma theophylline levels closely monitored.

88. J

The House Officer has presumably given vitamin K. A symptomatic patient with a high INR and a prosthetic heart valve should have a controlled reduction of the INR. If the INR drops below the required therapeutic level the patient is at risk of clots forming on the prosthetic valve, leading to valve failure and embolic phenomena. Reduction of the INR in these patients should be discussed with the Haematology Department.

89. E

Ciclosporin is a calcineurin inhibitor. It is may be used to suppress the immune system and has a major role in post-transplant immunosuppression to prevent and treat graft-versus-host disease. It is also markedly nephrotoxic and requires drug level monitoring to ensure a therapeutic range is achieved. Drugs such as quinolones (ciprofloxacin), vancomycin, co-trimoxazole and aminoglycosides increase the risk of ciclosporin toxicity. Macrolides directly increase plasma ciclosporin levels.

90. B

Digoxin toxicity may produce cardiac arrhythmias or heart block. Hypokalaemia caused by a potent loop diuretic may predispose a patient to digoxin toxicity. Normally, correction of the electrolyte disturbance and withdrawal of digoxin will correct the situation. For those with life-threatening digoxin overdose, specific digoxin antibodies may be given.

91. D

Cimetidine inhibits the renal elimination of metformin, leading to higher plasma levels. This in turn may lead to hypoglycaemia.

Theme: Urea and electrolytes

92. C

This lady is having runs of ventricular tachycardia and has an associated low blood pressure. Both ACE inhibitors and spironolactone promote sodium excretion and potassium retention. This may lead to hyperkalaemia, which predisposes to ventricular arrhythmias. Her treatment should include calcium ions to stabilise the myocardium and an insulin and dextrose infusion to promote the cellular uptake of intravascular potassium.

93. D

This elderly gentleman has rhabdomyolysis secondary to pressure necrosis of his muscles, caused by the prolonged period of lying on the hard floor. His CK is high, due to its release from damaged muscle cells. Treatment must ensure adequate hydration is maintained to prevent renal failure, and treatment of hyperkalaemia. A cause for the initial fall must also be sought.

94. A

This patient has hypokalaemia as a result of diarrhoea. He has been able to maintain hydration. Severe hypokalaemia causes muscle weakness, a decreased-amplitude ECG, a prolonged QT interval and, in extreme circumstances, it may lead to asystolic cardiac arrest.

95. D

This fit young soldier has developed rhabdomyolysis secondary to severe muscular exercise. Other causes include trauma, including prolonged pressure, and statin therapy for hypercholesterolaemia.

96. F

This patient has acute pancreatitis. Serum amylase is usually greatly elevated. Patients are in severe pain, requiring opioid analgesia, and in cardiovascular shock, resulting in a raised urea. They have a raised white cell count, and increased blood glucose levels reflecting reduced pancreatic function. They also exhibit an acute fall in serum albumin with a consequent fall in serum calcium.

97. E

This patient has hyperosmolar non-ketotic coma (HONK). It is a condition that signifies a type 2 diabetic (non-insulin-dependent diabetes mellitus, NIDDM) emergency. Severe hyperglycaemia leads to profound dehydration and patients develop a hyperosmolar state (osmolality = $2([Na^+] + [K^+]) + [Glu] + [Ur]$). However, there is no ketosis in contrast to the diabetic emergency of ketoacidosis seen in type 1 diabetics. Due to the hyperosmolar state, patients often have a decreased level of consciousness on presentation.

Theme: Mental Health Act

98. G
99. A
100. A
101. I
102. B

Section 2: Compulsory admission for assessment (or for assessment followed by appropriate medical treatment). Lasts 28 days. Two doctors (one who is section 12-approved, one who knows the patient) must agree that the patient has a mental disorder that requires the patient to be detained in hospital. Application is by a close relative or an approved social worker.

Section 3: Compulsory admission for treatment for up to six months. Patient must have a known mental disorder. Application is by an approved social worker. Two doctors required to support (one who is section 12-approved).

Section 4: Compulsory admission for assessment in an emergency. Valid for 72 hours only. Application is by a close relative or an approved social worker. One doctor required to support.

Section 5: Detention order applicable to any inpatient. Valid for 72 hours. Application is usually by the consultant in charge of patient's care.

Section 136: A police officer may remove to a 'place of safety', for assessment, any person found in a public place who appears to be suffering from a mental disorder.

Common law: A doctor may initiate emergency treatment if a patient is incapable of rational thought and they are unable to comprehend the medical nature of their situation. This frequently occurs if the patient is under the influence of alcohol or drugs or suffering from a psychiatric disorder.

No action: Any patient may decline life-saving treatment provided that they fulfil the following criteria:
- They understand the information given regarding proposed treatment and the consequences of declining treatment.
- They believe the information given.
- They are able to weigh up the information and arrive at a choice.

Theme: Headache

103. H

This is usually a disorder of the elderly. There is enlargement of the cerebral ventricles without an increase in the CSF pressure. It commonly presents with dementia, ataxia and urinary incontinence.

104. F

This is an AIDS-defining illness. It occurs in patients with a low CD4 count. It often has a slowly-evolving prodromal phase with fever, malaise and headache. Patients may have nausea, vomiting and photophobia and neck stiffness at the time of presentation. Indian-ink staining of CSF shows *Cryptococcus neoformans*. Treatment is with the intravenous antifungal agents, amphotericin and/or flucytosine. *Molluscum contagiosum* is a good indicator of immunosupression in HIV infection.

105. J

This patient has had a spontaneous bleed into the subarachnoid space. It classically presents with very severe headache of sudden onset. The initial pain is often in the occipital region. Patients may remain well or be very seriously ill on presentation. Diagnosis is by CT scan or lumbar puncture if the CT scan is negative and no focal lesion is demonstrated. It is often associated with underlying saccular (berry) aneurysms or arteriovenous (AV) malformations.

106. A

This girl has bacterial meningitis. She has the classic signs of fever, headache and neck stiffness. Photophobia and vomiting are often present. Meningococcal (*Neisseria meningitidis*) meningitis should be immediately suspected. There may or may not be a petechial rash. Cefotaxime/ceftriaxone therapy should be commenced as soon as possible if meningococcus is thought likely. This disease may show rapid progression from fully well to obtunded and septicaemic and the value of early antibiotics cannot be underestimated. Lumbar puncture should be avoided.

107. E

This is caused by slow bleeding from a vein into the subdural space. Gradually symptoms result from haematoma accumulation over a period of days or weeks. There may be headache, reduced mental capacity or more focal signs. The elderly and alcohol abusers are at highest risk but trauma is also a cause in any age group.

108. C

This uncommon disorder often occurs in overweight women. It represents an increase in CSF pressure without an increase in the size of the cerebral ventricles. It causes headache and visual blurring due to papilloedema. It may be associated with steroids and tetracycline therapy. Thiazide diuretics and acetazolamide may be useful in management. Weight reduction may also be helpful.

Theme: ECG

109. G

Digoxin toxicity may present with nausea, anorexia, visual disturbance or cardiac arrhythmias. Complete atrioventricular block and ventricular tachycardia are the more serious manifestations. The so-called 'reversed tick'-ST segment depression may be seen on the 12-lead ECG along with first-degree heart block – these do not necessarily indicate toxicity.

110. D

This abnormal pattern of conduction through the AV node is also known as 'Wenckebach' type. The AV node becomes increasingly refractory to conduction, with an increasing PR interval on the ECG, until there is complete failure of conduction across the AV node and a QRS complex is dropped. Ischaemic heart disease and fibrosis of the conduction fibres in the elderly are the commonest causes.

111. I

This may be a congenital condition but is more commonly caused by ischaemic or infiltrative disease. There is an rSR′ pattern in lead V_1 and prominent S waves in leads I and V_6. The QRS complex is widened (> 100 ms).

112. F

The QT interval represents the time taken for a complete cycle of ventricular depolarisation and repolarisation. Prolongation may be a congenital defect (Romano–Ward syndrome) but more commonly is an acquired defect. Many drugs, including phenthiozines, macrolides, quinolones and class III antiarrhythmic drugs, cause QT prolongation. Hypokalaemia and bradycardia are also important causes. Excessive QT-interval prolongation predisposes to torsades de pointes or polymorphic ventricular tachycardia.

113. H

The normal QRS axis on the 12-lead ECG is –30° to +90°. An axis of +150° represents right axis deviation. Causes include left posterior hemiblock, right ventricular hypertrophy, acute right ventricular strain (eg pulmonary embolism) and right bundle branch block.

114. A

This patient has Wolff–Parkinson–White syndrome. He has an accessory pathway between his atria and ventricles. This allows conduction of the electrical impulse through both the AV node and the accessory pathway. The delta wave represents premature activation of the ventricles via the accessory pathway. This abnormal situation can give rise to runs of tachycardia with anterograde conduction through the AV node and retrograde conduction through the accessory pathway creating an electrical loop.

Theme: Acute hot knee

115. C

This is a form of septic arthritis, although at the time of presentation the joint fluid may be sterile – *Neisseria gonorrhoeae* may still be cultured from the genital tract. Usually the patient has recovered from the initial pyrexial phase and characteristic rash affecting the palms and soles prior to the onset of the large-joint mono/polyarticular arthritis. Treatment involves ciprofloxacin or tetracyclines.

116. F

This represents acute inflammation of the pre-patellar bursa. The bursa is inflamed and tender, often with a large degree of swelling. It can be caused by excessive kneeling – 'housemaid's knee'. NSAIDs and avoidance of mechanical aggravation are the primary treatment.

117. H

This lady has a monoarticular swelling secondary to underlying systemic disease. Commonly the small joints of the hand are the worst affected but a monoarticular presentation in a large joint may occur. In rheumatoid arthritis both ESR and CRP are raised during active disease. In SLE only the ESR is elevated.

118. G

This represents an acute synovitis initiated by calcium pyrophosphate crystal deposition in the joint. It often affects elderly women and is very painful. In younger people it may be associated with underlying pathology – Wilson's disease, hyperparathyroidism or haemochromatosis. The crystals seen from the joint aspirate in gout (sodium urate) are negatively birefringent under polarised light.

119. I

Staphlococcus aureus is the commonest cause of septic arthritis. In children *Haemophilus influenzae* must also be considered. Occasionally, other Gram-negative organisms may be involved. The infected joint is hot, swollen and very painful, and usually held in a fixed position as a result of spasm in the surrounding muscles. The patient is usually pyrexial and blood cultures are often positive. Joint aspirate is turbid and should be sent for microscopy and culture. A joint washout and systemic antibiotics are required.

Theme: Full blood count

120. C

This patient has polycythaemia rubra vera. This is a stem cell disorder resulting in increased haemoglobin and an increased packed cell volume. The WCC is raised in about 70% of cases and the platelet count in about 50%. Patients may present with tiredness, depression or visual disturbance. Itching after taking a hot bath is common. Thrombosis and haemorrhage are the major complications.

121. D

This lady has thrombocytopenia secondary to heparin therapy. This is an immune-mediated reaction against heparin/platelet factor 4 complexes. All heparins may cause this reaction although it is less common with low molecular weight heparins. Paradoxically, thrombosis is the major risk and all heparin must be discontinued.

122. A

This lady has pancytopenia caused by the carbimazole. Carbimazole may also cause agranulocytosis. The Committee for the Safety of Medicines recommends that a WCC be performed on any patient with signs of infection who is taking carbimazole. Propylthiouracil (also used for the treatment of hyperthyroidism) may also cause pancytopenia.

123. E

Post-splenectomy patients have a raised platelet count for two to three weeks. This may be persistent in up to 30% of cases. This leads to an increased risk of thromboembolic events. Splenectomy is usually performed for trauma, haemolytic anaemias, autoimmune thrombocytopenic purpura and hypersplenism.

124. A

This boy has aplastic anaemia secondary to parvovirus infection (B19 subtype). The rash on his face represented the 'slapped cheek' appearance of erythema infectiosum or 'fifth disease'. This is common in schoolchildren. Other viruses that may cause aplastic anaemia include EBV, HIV and the hepatitis viruses.

Theme: Advanced paediatric life support

125. A

The child is lying in a main road. You may be at high risk of injury if you do not stop to assess whether it is safe to approach.

126. F

The child is unconscious with meningococcal septicaemia. She is unable to maintain her own airway. The grunting represents expiration through a partially closed airway. With all assessment 'airway' is the starting point. Lifting the chin may alleviate part of the respiratory difficulty. Clearly the child needs definitive airway management through intubation until recovery.

127. I

This child has obvious burns but also has evidence of trauma. Playing in a condemned house should also raise the suspicion of potential trauma. As his breathing is deteriorating, his airway ('A-B-C') needs to be assessed. Therefore he needs a controlled airway assessment with cervical immobilisation because of the risk of spinal injury.

128. E

This boy is likely to have a haemopneumothorax. An X-ray would confirm this. His airway is patent and his cardiovascular system is stable. A traumatic pneumothorax is treated with a chest drain.

129. F

Having made the assessment of unresponsiveness you need to assess whether or not the child is breathing. The airway should be opened and the mouth inspected for potential obstructing objects. Holding your face close to the child's mouth, you listen and feel for exhalation and look across the child's chest for signs of movement. This should be done for 10 seconds.

130. H

In this child, talking tells you the airway is patent. Breathing is laboured and giving supplemental oxygen may significantly improve the situation or at least prevent further deterioration.

Theme: Chest pain

131. A

Cocaine causes agitation, tachycardia, hypertension, arrhythmias and coronary artery spasm. Coronary artery spasm may lead to angina-type chest pain and even myocardial infarction.

132. B

Dissection of the aorta within the chest causes severe central pain, usually radiating through to the back between the scapulae. It is an uncommon presentation to the Emergency Department. It is associated with hypertension and collagen disorders (Marfan's syndrome, pseudoxanthoma elasticum). Late-stage syphilis is also a cause.

133. J

This lady has embolised a clot from her leg and infarcted her lung. Antiphospholipid syndrome predisposes to recurrent thromboses. The clinical presentation of a pulmonary embolism (PE) ranges from mild pleuritic chest pain to cardiac arrest. Often patients are mildly short of breath and hypoxic on arterial blood gas testing and D-dimer testing will be positive. Chest X-rays are often normal. Diagnosis is by ventilation/perfusion scanning or spiral CT.

134. K

This disorder is caused by inflammation around the costosternal junctions. It may be bilateral or unilateral and the chest wall is very tender over the affected area. Reassurance and NSAIDs are the mainstay of treatment.

135. D

This patient has long-standing pleural plaques, a sign of significant previous asbestos exposure. Asbestos has many negative effects on the lung, including pleural thickening (plaques), pleural effusions, lung fibrosis and mesothelioma. It is also associated with carcinoma of the bronchus. No medical therapy is known to alter the progress of asbestos-related disease.

136. C

This lady has reflux of gastric contents into the oesophagus, the acid nature of which is irritating the oesophageal mucosa and causing pain. This is often an indigestion-type pain, which may be relieved by antacids or proton pump inhibitors. Obesity, fatty foods, alcohol, cigarette smoking and large meals are associated. Complications include oesophageal stricture and Barrett's oesophagus.

Theme: Asthma

137. I

This is defined by a peak expiratory flow rate (PEFR) 50–75% of predicted and no features of severe asthma.

138. E

The first-line treatment for asthma is immediate high-concentration oxygen followed by nebulised salbutamol (or terbutaline) and ipratropium bromide. These will help mediate bronchodilation (action on β_2-receptors) and reduce bronchial secretions (anticholinergic action). If the patient is deteriorating on nebulised therapy, intravenous magnesium is recommended in the BTS guidelines to initiate bronchodilatation.

139. K

As above – after oxygen therapy is commenced, a nebuliser should be given. Although near-fatal asthma requires sedation, intubation and ventilation, this always takes time to initiate.

140. H

Any one of the following defines life-threatening asthma:

- PEFR < 33% of predicted
- $Pa\text{O}_2$ < 8 kPa
- oxygen saturation < 92%
- normal $Pa\text{CO}_2$
- silent chest
- cyanosis
- feeble respiratory effort
- bradycardia, dysrhythmia, hypotension
- exhaustion, confusion, coma.

141. G

Any patient with a raised $Pa\text{CO}_2$ has near-fatal asthma. They require sedation, intubation and ventilation as definitive management but all other therapies should also be commenced.

Theme: Red blood cells

142. F

Vitamin B_{12} deficiency causes a megaloblastic anaemia. Vitamin B_{12} is found in animal products but not in plants – it cannot be synthesised by humans. Therefore, both diet and the ability to absorb vitamin B_{12} are factors to consider if deficiency exists. Pernicious anaemia is caused by atrophy of the gastric mucosa with subsequent reduction in production of intrinsic factor, which is required for the absorption of vitamin B_{12} in the ileum.

143. A

These are damaged red blood cells, which have subsequently resealed their cell membrane. They are incomplete and misshapen. Causes include prosthetic heart valves, renal dialysis and micro-angiopathic haemolytic anaemias.

144. H

Sickle cell patients suffer crises which may be spontaneous or initiated by intercurrent infection, cold or hypoxia. Sickling of red blood cells in small vessels may cause severe pain in almost any site. Chest pain and bone pain are common. Priapism is also seen. Patients may also suffer severe neurological sequelae and hyposplenism through recurrent splenic infarcts.

145. C

This patient has Felty's syndrome – rheumatoid arthritis (RA) with hypersplenism and pancytopenia. Any cause of chronic splenic enlargement may cause hypersplenism.

146. I

Lead poisoning leads to inhibition of enzymes involved in haem synthesis, causing anaemia. It also inhibits enzymes that disperse excess RNA and results in abnormal staining of red blood cells on a blood film (discrete blue particles – stippling effect)

147. B

This patient has iron deficiency anaemia. This can result from blood loss, poor dietary intake or decreased absorption. Hookworm infestation of the duodenum is the commonest infective cause worldwide.

Theme: Management of cardiac arrest

148. C

The management of pulseless ventricular tachycardia (VT) is the same as for VF. Defibrillation at 200 J is advised as soon as possible. Do not waste time attending to the airway, or giving drugs.

149. J

Immediate needle thoracocentesis is the treatment for tension pneumothorax. There are a number of causes of cardiac arrest, especially presenting with pulseless electrical activity, that may be reversible. These are remembered as the four 'H's and the four 'T's: hypoxia, hypothermia, hypovolaemia and hyperkalaemia; tension pneumothorax, tamponade, thromboembolic and toxins/drugs.

150. K

A precordial thump is advised in a witnessed and monitored arrest when the patient is in VF. The thump delivers a small shock to the heart of a few joules.

151. E

The outcome from out-of-hospital arrest is very poor, especially if the rhythm is asystole. Intubation and ventilation with high-flow oxygen will correct hypoxia.

152. H

Intravenous adrenaline (epinephrine) is recommended every three to five minutes in cardiac arrest.

153. F

If a patient remains in VF after one shock then this is repeated a fast as possible to a total of three shocks. However, if VF converts to asystole (or PEA) then no shock is appropriate. CPR should be continued. No drugs should be given as the myocardium may be stunned after a shock and adrenaline could be harmful. Adrenaline should be given after one minute of CPR if asystole persists.

154. C

The VF algorithm advises the first three shocks to be at 200 J, 200 J, then 360 J, with all subsequent shocks at 360 J, unless there has been a return in output in which case you revert to 200 J.

Theme: Basic life support management

155. B

In a paediatric cardiac arrest the recommendation is first to open the airway, then to check breathing. If the child is not breathing then two effective rescue breaths are given. After this, check a central pulse. If this is absent then external cardiac massage is started. Alternate breaths and cardiac massage at a ratio of 1 : 5. Continue for one minute. After this you must obtain access to advanced life support. You may be able to carry a child to a telephone if no one else has summoned help. In reality, in a supermarket help will be on its way. In this case you continue CPR until help arrives or you become exhausted.

156. E

The most likely cause of a respiratory arrest in this adult patient is a cardiac arrest. The best chance of a successful outcome is if the patient is in VF and is electrically defibrillated. In this situation you are advised to leave the patient to find the nearest defibrillator rather than start rescue breaths.

157. G

Groaning implies a return of spontaneous breathing and also requires an adequate circulation. However, he has a reduced level of consciousness. If he is lying on his back there is a danger of the tongue blocking the airway so he should be placed in the recovery position.

158. A

There are a number of causes, but disconnection, accidental extubation or blockage of the endotracheal tube must be looked for.

159. E

Drowning would be an indication to start CPR rather than leaving the patient to summon help and a defibrillator. Drowning and hypothermia may require prolonged resuscitation attempts. If there has been no response to initial CPR then leave the patient to get help. In an adult who may have sustained trauma or whose condition indicates drowning as the cause of cardiac arrest, the first action is to give one minute of CPR prior to leaving to summon help.

160. E

Your own safety is at risk. There is no merit in becoming another victim.

Theme: Management of poisoning

161. D

Flumazenil is used to reverse the sedating effects of benzodiazepines. It should not be used in a patient with chronic benzodiazepine use as it may induce dangerous withdrawal.

162. H

Morphine is often prescribed in too high doses in the elderly. The opiate antagonist naloxone can be given intravenously or intramuscularly.

163. I

Although flumazenil will reverse benzodiazepine poisoning its use is not recommended to reverse overdose. If the patient is benzodiazepine-dependent then flumazenil will induce withdrawal, including fits, which will be difficult to manage. Also there is a risk of arrhythmias associated with tricyclic antidepressants.

164. E

Glucagon mobilises glycogen stores in the liver to release glucose. It can be given intramuscularly which is safe and easy to perform, hence its popularity in the pre-hospital setting. Glucose should not be given orally in the context of a reduced level of consciousness.

165. E

First-line inotropes will not work if the β-receptors are blocked. Glucagon bypasses this problem, given as a bolus of a few milligrams intravenously, then as an infusion.

Theme: Child with a painful leg

166. F

Perthes disease generally presents with limp, with or without pain, between the ages of four and eight years. Avascular necrosis of the femoral head occurs followed by replacement with new bone. The patient can be left with residual femoral head deformity. Other causes of avascular necrosis in children are sickle cell disease and prolonged steroid use. This is unlikely to be sickle cell disease as this would be associated with severe pain and there would have been a history of other crises by the age of five.

167. J

Slipped upper femoral epiphysis can present with pain and a limp of gradual onset, or more acutely after minor trauma. It presents at this age and classically in obese boys with delayed secondary sexual development.

168. D

This is a traction apophysitis at the insertion of the patella tendon into the tibial tubercle. Tenderness over the tubercle and X-ray changes confirm the diagnosis. Treatment involves reducing the strain at this site by stopping sports or by immobilisation.

169. B

In this age group the joint may become inflamed after an upper respiratory tract infection. The exact cause is not known but it causes an irritable hip or transient synovitis. Blood tests and X-rays are normal. Most cases resolve in a few days or weeks. This diagnosis is only made once all investigations are demonstrated to be normal.

170. C

The pathological diagnosis is likely to be fractured femur. However, the clinical diagnosis may be non-accidental injury. Infants are unlikely to break their bones without some external force. Children may be brought in by carers other than the parents. A senior paediatric opinion must be sought immediately while you attend to the child's injury.

Theme: Blood gas analysis

171. A

A base excess more negative than –2 is a metabolic acidosis as in this case. A base excess more positive than +2 is a metabolic alkalosis. This patient is hyperventilating to try to compensate for the metabolic acidosis. Diabetic ketoacidosis would be the commonest cause.

172. E

This patient is also hyperventilating, which has pushed the blood oxygen above normal and made him mildly alkalotic. There is no hypoxia or metabolic acidosis so no evident reason for the hyperventilation.

173. F

This patient is also hyperventilating but is still hypoxic. This implies a problem with gas exchange in the lungs and an increased ventilation/perfusion ratio mismatch. Pneumonia would be a common cause, but a normal chest X-ray would make pulmonary embolism the likely cause.

174. G

In a moderate asthma attack, the carbon dioxide is low as the patient hyperventilates; as the patient deteriorates and tires the carbon dioxide becomes normal and then raised. This patient is in danger of respiratory arrest.

Theme: Management of common injuries in the Emergency Department

175. D

The most likely diagnosis is a traumatic shoulder dislocation. An X-ray should be taken before reduction to confirm the diagnosis and after reduction to confirm success.

176. B

This could be managed as above, but recurrent dislocations from minor trauma can usually be easily and quickly reduced. No X-ray is needed before or after this procedure.

177. A

This is an emergency as the longer the fracture dislocation is left the worse the outcome. This should be reduced under analgesia and conscious sedation and immobilised in plaster before X-ray.

178. B

This is a clinical diagnosis and fracture would be very unlikely from a simple yawn. This is reduced by placing your gloved fingers inside the patient's mouth and pushing down and back on the lower molars, usually without any sedation. There is no need for X-ray.

179. B

There is no indication to X-ray a fractured nose in the Emergency Department. Minor deformity is often due to asymmetric swelling and will go when the swelling resolves. Ear, nose and throat (ENT) surgeons will reduce the fracture if needed seven to ten days after the injury.

180. B

A fractured toe is a clinical diagnosis and will heal with conservative management. Nothing is gained by X-ray.

Theme: Management of pneumothorax

181. D

This is not an immediate emergency. Needle aspiration should be performed under sterile conditions. A large-bore cannula is inserted into the second intercostal space, mid-clavicular line, and the air is aspirated to dryness. If this is successful the patient is discharged with X-ray follow-up.

182. C

This is an emergency as the patient has evidence of a tension pneumothorax. Air will hiss out under pressure through the cannula. After this immediate treatment, a chest drain must be inserted.

183. A

Unlike a spontaneous pneumothorax, needle aspiration is not recommended in trauma. A chest drain should be inserted. The recommended site is in the fifth intercostal space, mid-axillary line.

184. A

Aspiration has failed and the next step is a chest drain.

185. A

This is an open pneumothorax. The initial management is a dressing taped on three sides over the hole to act as a valve and only let air out. A chest drain should be inserted (not through the wound) and then the wound can be closed.

186. E

There is nothing to be gained from aspiration, and he should just be monitored as an outpatient with X-rays. Advise not to fly or dive and to return if the situation deteriorates. A check X-ray should be performed at 48 hours, or sooner if he returns with increasing symptoms.

Theme: Diagnosis of rashes

187. E

This is a classic site. The lesions can be violet in colour and develop a fine white network on their surface called Wickham's striae.

188. F

The initial lesion is called a herald patch. The condition is possibly of viral origin and usually spontaneously remits. The lesions are sometimes itchy and this can be treated with topical steroid.

189. G

This is a fungal infection of the trunk caused by *Malassezia furfur.* It is seen in Britain after sunbathing abroad. It causes depigmentation of tanned skin, but increased pigmentation of untanned skin. A topical imidazole such as miconazole cream can be used.

190. H

There are many presentations of psoriasis, the most common being classic plaque psoriasis. Apart from the skin, psoriasis can affect the scalp, the nails, and the joints.

191. C

Dermatitis herpetiformis will benefit from a gluten-free diet. Oral dapsone is also used.

Theme: Causes of a non-blanching rash

192. E

Henoch–Schönlein purpura is a hypersensitivity reaction, sometimes preceded by an upper respiratory tract infection. Associated problems include arthralgia, abdominal pain, and microscopic haematuria. Glomerulonephritis can progress to renal failure. The main treatment is analgesics.

193. F

This is an immune disorder characterised by platelet-bound antibody, often with a previous history of infection. Most episodes resolve over a few months but there is a danger of serious bleeding.

194. H

Always consider child abuse if the purpura are in an unusual place or show an unusual distribution.

195. G

Meningococcal purpura implies significant septicaemia. Rapid deterioration is likely. Aggressive management with antibiotics, intravenous fluids, intubation and ventilation is required.

196. A

The history suggests low haemoglobin and platelets as well as poor immunity. In leukaemia all three blood cell types are affected.

Theme: Endocrine disease

197. A

Primary hypoadrenalism due to destruction of the adrenal cortex leads to a reduction in glucocorticoid, mineralocorticoid and sex steroid production. Reduced cortisol levels produce an increase in adrenocorticotrophic hormone (ACTH) production by the pituitary, which is responsible for the pigmentation by its action on melanocytes. Postural hypotension is due to hypovolaemia and sodium loss.

198. C

Cushing's syndrome is due to an increase in glucocorticoids. An increase in ACTH from the pituitary is called Cushing's disease. Other causes are ACTH-producing tumours and non-ACTH dependent causes such as an adrenal adenoma.

199. B

Primary hyperaldosteronism causes sodium retention, hypertension and hypokalaemia. Conn's syndrome is due to an adrenal adenoma, but adrenal hyperplasia can also cause the condition.

200. G

Tumours that release noradrenaline and adrenaline (norepinephrine and epinephrine) frequently cause intermittent symptoms. Most phaechromocytomas arise from the adrenal glands. Some are associated with the multiple endocrine neoplasia syndromes.

REVISION CHECKLIST

The following themes have recently appeared in the PLAB Part 1 examination. Use this checklist in your revision.

General Medicine

- ❑ Anaemia
- ❑ Antibiotic prophylaxis
- ❑ Causes of acute breathlessness
- ❑ Causes of dysphagia
- ❑ Causes of immobility
- ❑ Causes of pneumonia
- ❑ Chest pain and its management
- ❑ Complications of anti-epileptic drugs
- ❑ Complications of diabetes
- ❑ Decision making in terminal care
- ❑ Diagnosis of acquired liver diseases
- ❑ Diagnosis of asthma
- ❑ Diagnosis of hypertension
- ❑ Diagnosis of infection
- ❑ Diagnosis of joint pain
- ❑ Diagnosis of shock
- ❑ Differential diagnosis of chest pain
- ❑ Haematological diagnosis
- ❑ Headaches
- ❑ HIV risk prevention
- ❑ Hypercalcaemia, treatment and causes
- ❑ Immediate treatment of meningitis/head injury
- ❑ Initial management of convulsions
- ❑ Investigation of chest pain
- ❑ Investigations for headaches
- ❑ Investigations relevant to urinary tract infections
- ❑ Malabsorption
- ❑ Management of arrhythmias
- ❑ Management of breast cancer
- ❑ Management of pain in terminal care
- ❑ Management of stroke/TIA
- ❑ Mechanism of poisoning
- ❑ Method of transmission of infection
- ❑ Pain relief
- ❑ Prescribing drugs in renal failure
- ❑ Prevention of jaundice and hepatitis
- ❑ Prevention and treatment of deep vein thrombosis

- ❑ Risk factors of injury in elderly
- ❑ Sudden loss of vision
- ❑ Swelling of legs
- ❑ Treatment of DVT
- ❑ Treatment of pancreatitis
- ❑ Treatment of pain relief in terminally ill patients
- ❑ Unconscious patient

Obstetrics and Gynaecology

- ❑ Antenatal screening
- ❑ Causes of incontinence
- ❑ Causes of vaginal bleeding and primary treatment
- ❑ Eclampsia and its management
- ❑ Investigations of amenorrhoea
- ❑ Investigation for ante-partum haemorrhage
- ❑ Investigations for vaginal bleeding during pregnancy
- ❑ Management of preeclampsia

Ophthalmology and ENT

- ❑ Diagnosis of earache
- ❑ Pain in the ear
- ❑ Prevention of deterioration of vision
- ❑ Sudden loss of vision
- ❑ Treatment of earache
- ❑ Treatment of red eye

Paediatrics

- ❑ Abdominal pain
- ❑ Acute vomiting in children
- ❑ Asthma
- ❑ Bleeding per vaginum
- ❑ Causes of vomiting
- ❑ Developmental delay
- ❑ Difficulty in walking
- ❑ Jaundice
- ❑ Non-accidental injuries
- ❑ Treatment of acute/chronic asthma
- ❑ Treatment of urinary tract infection

Psychiatry

- ❑ Acute confusional state
- ❑ Causes of dementia
- ❑ Differential diagnosis of confusion
- ❑ Diagnosis of depression
- ❑ Management of dementia
- ❑ Management of schizophrenia
- ❑ Psychiatric illness and its management
- ❑ Risk of suicide
- ❑ Treatment of alcoholics and drug abuse
- ❑ Treatment of psychosis

Surgery

- ❑ Antibiotic prophylaxis in surgical patients
- ❑ Complications of cholecystectomy
- ❑ Investigations of Acute abdomen
- ❑ Investigations in aortic aneurysm
- ❑ Investigations of a breast lump
- ❑ Investigations of chronic abdominal pain
- ❑ Management of burns
- ❑ Management of an ischaemic limb

INDEX

Locators refer to question number.

PASTEST – DEDICATED TO YOUR SUCCESS

PasTest has been publishing books for doctors for over 30 years. Our extensive experience means that we are always one step ahead when it comes to knowledge of current trends and content of the Royal College exams.

We use only the best authors and lecturers, many of whom are Consultants and Royal College Examiners, which enables us to tailor our books and courses to meet your revision needs. We incorporate feedback from candidates to ensure that our books are continually improved.

This commitment to quality ensures that students who buy a PasTest book or attend a PasTest course achieve successful exam results.

Delivery to your Door

With a busy lifestyle, nobody enjoys walking to the shops for something that may or may not be in stock. Let us take away the hassle and deliver direct to your door. We will despatch your book within 24 hours of receiving your order. We also offer free delivery on books for medical students to UK addresses.

How to Order:

www.pastest.co.uk

To order books safely and securely online, shop at our website.

Telephone: +44 (0)1565 752000

Fax: +44 (0)1565 650264

PasTest Ltd, FREEPOST, Knutsford, WA16 7BR.

PASTEST BOOKS FOR PLAB

PLAB Part 1 EMQ Pocket Books

Book 1 *1 901198 56 1*
Book 2 *1 901198 62 6*
Book 3 *1 901198 70 7*

Our series of PLAB Part 1 pocket books give candidates essential practice of extended matching questions which they will encounter in the Part 1 examination.

PLAB Part 2 Made Easy: OSCEs with discussion

E Mukherjee, J Treml *1 901198 92 8*

Covers procedures, trauma and orthopaedics, examinations, resuscitation, history taking, drugs, counselling, data interpretation, emergency management and communication.

Further titles to aid revision

OSCES for Medical Students Vol 1

A Feather J S P Lumley and R Visvanathan *1 904627 09 9*

Contains chapters on: Neurology, Psychiatry, ENT, Opthalmology, Endocrinology, Ethics & Law

OSCES for Medical Students Vol 2

A Feather J S P Lumley and R Visvanathan *1 904627 10 2*

Contains chapters on: Cardiovascular Systems, Haematology, Respiratory, Orthopaedics, Trauma, Rheumatology and Dermatology

OSCES for Medical Students Vol 3

A Feather J S P Lumley R Visvanathan & J Round *1 904627 11 0*

Contains chapters on: Gastroenterology, Hepatobiliary, Renal Medicine, Urology, Obstetrics & Gynaecology and Paediatrics

The Practical Guide to Medical Ethics and Law

C Baxter, M Brennan, Y Coldicott *1 901198 76 6*

Written by experts in the field of medical ethics and medical law, this book is aimed at junior doctors and medical students and will also appeal to law students.

100 Clinical Cases & OSCEs in Surgery
N Aherne, A Hill & E McDermott *1 904627 00 5*
It contains 100 OSCEs in system-based chapters written in a style that takes students through the OSCE stations. Each gives details of core knowledge, discussion points and advanced issues, and includes several X-rays, illustrations and checklists

100 Clinical Cases & OSCEs in Medicine
D McCluskey *1 904627 12 9*
Designed for final year medical students and PLAB 2 candidates this book contains 100 OSCEs!

USEFUL ADDRESSES

General Medical Council
178 Great Portland Street
London
W1N 6JE
Tel: 44 207 915 3481
Fax: 44 207 915 3558

First Application Service
e-mail: firstcontact@gmc-uk.org
PLAB Test Section
e-mail: plab@gmc-uk.org

British Medical Association
BMA House
Tavistock Square
London
WC1H 9JP
Tel: 44 207 387 4499
Fax: 44 207 383 6400
e-mail: info.web@bma.org.uk

Irish Medical Council
Lynne House
Portobello Course
Lower Ratmine Road
Dublin 6
Eire
Tel: 003 531 496 5588
Fax: 003 531 498 3102

PasTest Ltd
Egerton Court
Parkgate Estate
Knutsford
Cheshire
WA16 8DX
Tel: 44 (0)1565 752000
Fax: 44 (0)1565 650264
e-mail: enquiries@pastest.co.uk

National Advice Centre for Postgraduate Medical Education (NACPME)
Bridgewater House
58 Whitworth Street
Manchester
M1 6BB
Tel: 44 161 957 7218
Fax: 44 161 957 7029
e-mail: nacpme@britishcouncil.org
Website: www.britishcouncil.org

NACPME provides information in the following main areas:
Registration with the General Medical Council (EEA and non-EEA)
Professional and Linguistic Assessments Board (PLAB) test and categories of exemption
International English Language Testing System (IELTS)
Overseas Doctors Training Scheme (ODTS)
Specialist Training
General Information on: immigration, employment, postgraduate courses and Royal College examinations

NOTES